PRAISE FOR *GRACE FOR AMATEURS*

"*Grace for Amateurs* is that rare Christian book packed with humor, depth, kindness, intelligence, and inclusion. If you yearn to return to the heart of faith—boundless, agenda-less love—sit down with Burana. She'll make you laugh and restore your hope."

—GLENNON DOYLE
NEW YORK TIMES BESTSELLING AUTHOR OF
LOVE WARRIOR AND *CARRY ON, WARRIOR*

"The real miracle of *Grace for Amateurs* is that, somehow, Lily Burana manages to write about finding God without coming across as annoying, delusional, or holier-than-thou. She conjures a God who loves you at your absolute worst, a God who rewards you just for showing up and trying—even through heartache, even through doubt, even through frustration and tears. Burana's version of grace is not a moment of blinding light; it's a simple, stubborn insistence on believing, against all odds, in the transformative power of giving your love freely and treating what you already have as precious. Hers is an addictive, poetic, and deeply moving book about the long, slow walk toward peace and gratitude, and how even a humble mess like you might take that first step."

—HEATHER HAVRILESKY
"ASK POLLY" ADVICE COLUMNIST AND AUTHOR OF *HOW TO BE A
PERSON IN THE WORLD* AND *DISASTER PREPAREDNESS*

"Generous, humorous, lyrical, humane. A handbook on how to see yourself as a lily of the field, as a sparrow, as a part of the world that God so loved."

—PATRICIA LOCKWOOD
AUTHOR OF *PRIESTDADDY*

"Marrying heart with humor, and more than a little fire, *Grace for Amateurs* is a soul-baring book of spiritual renewal that will resonate with anyone who has found themselves angry, lost, or just plain bewildered about life. A righteous survival guide that broadens the meaning of true devotion."

—JILL SOLOWAY
DIRECTOR OF *TRANSPARENT*

"A religious book for people who would never be caught dead buying a religious book. Lily Burana brings her wit, warmth, and rebellious spirit to some of the deepest questions we face. Her stories are a powerful reminder of our human need for mystery—and glitter."

—SARAH HEPOLA
AUTHOR OF THE *NEW YORK TIMES* BESTSELLING
BLACKOUT: REMEMBERING THE THINGS I DRANK TO FORGET

"I. Love. This. Book. So. Much. *Grace for Amateurs* is a stealth dive into the chaotic, salvific blend of sacred and profane that is the essence of Christian faith. I say 'stealth' because it is so smart, so unflinchingly honest, and so snort-your-wine funny that you'll forget this is a user's manual. Anyone hoping to walk a path of faith with authenticity, courage, and wicked good humor should tuck Lily Burana's new book into their knapsack."

—REV. LIZ EDMAN
AUTHOR OF *QUEER VIRTUE: WHAT LGBTQ PEOPLE KNOW ABOUT
LIFE AND LOVE AND HOW IT CAN REVITALIZE CHRISTIANITY*

"In *Grace for Amateurs*, Lily Burana reflects on the grit and glitter of our lives. Each page reminds us that God visits through soaring birds, dark costumes, and imperfect mothers. Most of all, Burana's words whisper that we must pay attention to this achingly beautiful world."

—CAROL HOWARD MERRITT
PASTOR AND AUTHOR OF *HEALING SPIRITUAL WOUNDS*

GRACE *for* AMATEURS

GRACE *for* AMATEURS

FIELD NOTES ON A
JOURNEY BACK TO FAITH

LILY BURANA

W PUBLISHING GROUP

AN IMPRINT OF THOMAS NELSON

Published in Nashville, Tennessee, by W Publishing, an imprint of Thomas Nelson.

Thomas Nelson titles may be purchased in bulk for educational, business, fund-raising, or sales promotional use. For information, please e-mail SpecialMarkets@ThomasNelson.com.

Unless otherwise noted, Scripture quotations are taken from the ESV® Bible (The Holy Bible, English Standard Version®). Copyright © 2001 by Crossway, a publishing ministry of Good News Publishers. Used by permission. All rights reserved.

Scripture quotations marked NIV are from the Holy Bible, New International Version®, NIV®. Copyright © 1973, 1978, 1984, 2011 by Biblica, Inc.™ Used by permission of Zondervan. All rights reserved worldwide. www.Zondervan.com. The "NIV" and "New International Version" are trademarks registered in the United States Patent and Trademark Office by Biblica, Inc.™

Any Internet addresses, phone numbers, or company or product information printed in this book are offered as a resource and are not intended in any way to be or to imply an endorsement by Thomas Nelson, nor does Thomas Nelson vouch for the existence, content, or services of these sites, phone numbers, companies, or products beyond the life of this book.

ISBN 978-0-7180-9593-2 (eBook)
ISBN 978-0-7180-9598-7 (HC)

Library of Congress Cataloging-in-Publication Data
Library of Congress Control Number: 2017908299

Printed in the United States of America

17 18 19 20 21   LSC   10 9 8 7 6 5 4 3 2 1

For my better angels, and for my family—including you.

CONTENTS

CONTENTS

1

TAKING FLIGHT

The day I almost killed myself was the day my life began anew.

This was not as beautiful as it sounds—although the day itself was beautiful, punishingly so, the sky an aching, acetylene flame blue. The mountains outside my car windows rose in a deep summer green from the riverside, and the grassy highway margins were salted with small, white wildflowers. New York's Hudson Valley was staging, as naturalist John Muir would say, the grand show.

I was in the blackest of moods, speeding along the river roadway to meet my friend Lori for lunch at a local Mexican place. By now I was about six months into an outpatient mental health treatment program at Poughkeepsie's Saint Francis Hospital, feeling pretty ripped apart by, well, feeling. I spent every day bobbing in the dark current of depression, too tired to swim, and afraid of going under. Everything seemed impossible. Just walking to the end of the driveway to get the mail required effort. I was miserable and miserable to be around, dragging through the days like Job with a migraine.

Have you ever had a year so terrible the best you can say about it is that you survived? I'd had several in a row by then, a grey-tone stretch of time when the bottom dropped out of my emotional life and I dangled over dark water by a thread. I was faking it but barely making it. Meals were prepared, deadlines were (mostly) met, items on the to-do list checked off one by one.

My résumé looked okay: after years of wild living and wandering, I had settled into a house on a hill with a retired Army officer who had two lovely sons, and we paid our bills on time. But there were struggling people in my passable-on-paper family whom I couldn't help no matter what I did, a sense of dread and foreboding that I couldn't outpace no matter how hard I tried, and the question that crossed my mind every time I drove over a bridge: *What would it feel like to jump?*

Practiced in how to abide depression's deep fog, I kept my obligations to a minimum and took my meds with the religiosity of a true believer. Big Pharma, hear my prayer.

But a terrifying complication arose: my usual, reliable medication stopped working. I needed to do something drastic, and fast. If I didn't, I feared I would die.

Since depression had been a part of my life for years, I'd become shrewd about covering it up. Very few people knew I was struggling, and I blocked almost everyone out. I told myself I was lying for a just cause. As a child I'd been taught to sacrifice emotional truth on the altar of surface harmony. Go along to get along, and get going with the order of the day. The world didn't revolve around you and your problems, even if they were threatening to kill you.

I do not recommend this as a strategy for sane living.

The therapy I was doing at Saint Francis, called dialectical behavioral therapy, had whittled my negative thoughts to a painfully clarified point. Originated by Marsha Linehan as a kind of hands-on, sort-out-that-mess-in-your-head treatment for people with borderline personality disorder, dialectical behavioral therapy is a modality that demands, essentially, a forensic investigation of what triggers outsize emotional reactions—rage, dissociation, destructive impulses, binging, or addictive behavior—in hopes of figuring out how to prevent further episodes. I didn't have BPD; mine was an unremarkable generalized anxiety disorder diagnosis, garnished with depression, a little post-traumatic stress, and occasional suicidal ideation. I was your garden-variety Nervous Nelly with the recurring urge to kill herself, but DBT helped me as much as it helped the other patients in my group: the lovely, chatty, older black woman with the dissociative identity disorder who let me hold her parakeet on my finger when she brought it to group one Wednesday; the temperamental recovering drunk bussed over from her halfway house, whose large statement earrings jangled as she spoke of the anger and pain of her twenty-nine years; the father who looked like an Aryan henchman with a farmboy smile, who had twin toddlers and a bipolar I diagnosis; and the fashionable young blonde who had, she told us as she tapped notes on her pink laptop, jumped from the roof of her apartment building and survived. Each week, we'd analyze the trigger sheets we'd filled in to examine what flawed, negative thinking was behind our acting out—no lying, no faking, no covering up.

It was such a relief. I could show up broken, and for two hours of unfettered honesty, not have to pretend to be okay.

The trigger analysis allowed me to look at how depression worked with, and on, my thinking. Depression is a funhouse, with suicidal ideation the wavy, distorting mirrors that have you trapped and stumbling from corner to corner in that box on the midway. You don't think clearly, and the first thing to disappear is your sense of worth. You believe you don't matter. You believe you'd be better off dead.

When someone dies by their own hand, those left behind spin in wonder: Didn't they know how loved they were? How valued? How much of a smoking crater they left behind by dying?

Well, no, they don't.

When you're in the funhouse of depression, the opposite becomes true. A deep, pervasive sense of worthlessness seeps across everything like a spreading stain. You fixate on the burden of your incapacity, how messed up and heavy you are, and there's no talking yourself out of it. You can't pull yourself up by your bootstraps because you don't have bootstraps. You don't even have boots. You're treading barefoot over broken glass, day after day, exhausted and sick of the pain. You can't seem to get it right, and you imagine how things would go much better, people would do so much better, if you weren't around to drag them down. You'd be doing everyone a favor, really.

That's how dangerous depression can be. Not only do you believe you'd be better off dead, but also that everyone else would be relieved by your absence. Good riddance to bad rubbish.

That day, that pretty day that did nothing to announce its fatefulness, saw me driving along this scenic Hudson Valley road, praying to see, feel, or hear God in any way. What I wanted was a miracle. More than anything, I wanted to know that my life mattered enough to save.

I decided to pray for that miracle. God meets us where we are, I had heard. *Well, here I am*, I thought, despondent, desperate, and flaming pissed.

It is said that if you want an honest relationship with God, you must relate to God honestly. We're beseeched to be truthful. Be authentic. *Okay, then, I'm gonna let it rip. Eat your Wheaties, Jesus, because it's about to get real.*

I delivered unto Jesus something less like a prayer and more like a harangue.

"God," I said aloud, "if you're listening, I want you to know that I think you're a fraud and a liar and a holdout. I am going to give you one chance, right now. Today. You're the almighty healer? Show me what you've got. Bring your A-game, big shot."

The bald eagle was making a comeback in the Hudson Valley. Taking the train down to the city in the winter, I'd seen dozens of them perched in the bare trees or diving into the river for fish. Sometimes a half dozen of them in a single trip. Since my ride to meet Lori would have me driving along the river for ten miles or so, I figured it wasn't too much to ask God to send me an eagle. It was simple: all I needed to see, I told myself, was one single bald eagle on this drive to let me know God was listening.

"Surely you can pull that off, Mister Man?" I said. "Sending down one puny eagle? For me?"

I sped along the river road, my eyes cast upward, looking for my eagle. My sign. *Any second now, God,* I thought. *If you don't show up, then I check out. You are a nonentity, and soon I will be too.*

I drove and I cursed God until I was breathless. This wasn't like any prayer I had ever prayed and certainly unlike anything I'd ever heard in church. I imagined Jesus himself, holding out a stop-sign hand: "Dude, seriously. Language." This was not my finest moment. But it surely was among my most sincere.

Chip away a certain type of rage, and what lies beneath is wild, desperate fear. My fear was based on the recent realization that my competent adult self was a fraud, and I didn't know who or what lay underneath. If I wasn't cloaked in perfectionism or the performance of a rebel stance, who was I? I was so pulled apart, I sat in a conference room in the mental health wing of a hospital a couple times a week to try to get it back together again. I was a mess.

Was I a mess worth saving? I put the answer in God's hands.

In retrospect, this seems a reckless and foolish thing to do. But reckless and foolish felt like my allies in this dismal, desperate state, and I figured, what did I have to lose besides my life?

As I got to the bend in the road where the Bear Mountain Bridge spans a narrow point in the Hudson, I still hadn't seen an eagle. I looked left to right across the horizon. Zip. Nada. I guess I had my answer. I wasn't worth a miracle.

Thanks for nothing, God.

Oh, and PS: Go screw yourself.

As I sped up the hill on the other side of the river, my energy flagged. I wasn't angry anymore; I was just sad. I wasn't worth it. I knew it.

About two miles away from the river, where the highway winds up a steep slope that would take me into Highland Falls, I looked ahead up the hill and caught the bright blue rim of noon sky framed by the windshield. In the luminous, cloudless sky-space between the canopy of trees on either side of the road flew a bald eagle, the shape of its dark wings and body stark against the blue, the white head and tail unmistakable. The eagle was flying east to west above me, slowly; then it banked around and flew back the other way, never exiting my field of vision. It seemed to be flying an elliptical circuit for my eyes only.

I was seeing exactly what I had prayed for. If I'd read it in a novel, it would strain credibility and fail the test of suspended disbelief. I'd have thrown the book across the room. The hackwork hand of God.

I was uplifted, but I was also furious. Furious because God had let me get so close to killing myself; furious even more because of what had happened, what I had seen: an eagle appearing as if God had willed it. I had worked for years to build skepticism into a fortress to keep myself safe, and it had been kicked over like a sandcastle by a cosmic thug.

The bully God had spoken.

Relief washed through me then—ask and ye shall receive! But that relief was shot through with fear: What did this mean? Was it a miracle? Or was I crazy?

It all came down to one word: *maybe.*

Maybe was the word that pulled me back, hateful and staggering, from the ledge.

Maybe I was crazy, but then . . .

Maybe it was a miracle.

Maybe I could believe.

Maybe God was the rock at rock bottom.

My heart felt positively nuked, my long-held, lone-wolf assumptions blown to bits, but there was a light-footed presence winding through all that smoking wreckage. It wasn't as though I envisioned a white-haired, bearded sky-daddy riding on a cloud, or Jesus hitchhiking at the side of the road; rather I sensed a formless, invisible, companionate energy, cruising slowly and obviously on a draft above my head. I thought about *Hamlet*: "There are more things in heaven and earth . . . than are dreamt of in your philosophy."[1]

Then I thought, *Holy crap, holy crap, holy crap.*

I pulled up to the restaurant and sat in the car, stunned and staring at the steering wheel for a few minutes. Then I went inside, where the colorful curled streamers hung from the ceiling and piped-in mariachi music brought me back to the present.

Lori sat at a corner table under an elaborate mural of Mayan pyramids. When she stood to hug me, I knew I looked as if I'd seen a ghost—or worse, as if I had seen God.

I have always relied upon Lori to be my official voice of reason, as she offers the impressive professional breadth of being both a licensed therapist and a practicing attorney. For years she's been listening to me amid the slog of depression with the perfect balance of concern and acceptance—urging me to get help while not pushing me at a pace I couldn't match. She is nothing if not steel-belted sane.

As I numbly shoved corn chips into my mouth, I told Lori what had happened, and she considered what I was saying without recoiling, or worse, laughing. Then with her attorney's calm, she said, "Dude, I'm not really a person who believes in signs, but I'd say that's a sign."

We folded up in familiar conversation—her family, mine, work, travel. With our usual retinue of lunch hour topics, I felt I was back in the earthly realm. The tale of the eagle had not derailed us. She didn't think I was a freak for telling her, and I didn't feel like a freak for having told. Martin Buber said, "When two people relate to each other authentically and humanly, God is the electricity that surges between them."[2]

Our lunch was served, and I ate way too much. As much as seeing the eagle felt weirdly exciting, it also gave me a feeling of being on the edge of dark woods. I'd better fill up for the journey just in case. I'm the type who believes in greeting any possible life change with a clean plate. I liked the idea of being fed with the food of the Spirit, but it paled in comparison to corn chips, which were right in front of me, inarguable in that paper-lined basket. I like my comforts tangible and preferably deep-fried.

In the parking lot, Lori and I hugged and kissed and said I love you as we always do. That's the best thing about old friends, that mooring of easy affection. A red dot pinned to the map of the heart: *You are here.* I drove away from lunch, overfullness billowing uncomfortably inside of me.

I remember learning as a child the Bible verse saying that we walk by faith, not by sight. And yet, sometimes you have to see to believe. Now I had.

Be careful what you pray for. I had prayed at the top of my lungs for a sign that I was worthy, and I got one.

Well, now what? There wasn't an angel chorus or the clear piercing note of Gideon's trumpet or even a low hippie thrum of *om*.

The interior of the car was terrifyingly, amazingly quiet. I was slowly accepting that I might have had my life saved by a miracle. But what did it mean?

The answer that arose was the most dangerous I could think of, and it would come to shape my life: *I don't know.*

I didn't know what the future would hold. I didn't know how my life would be molded by other hands, should I allow that to happen, and I didn't know if I had the patience or fortitude to hang on faithfully while I found out.

Were I to view the appearance of the eagle not as a miracle but an experiment, the result would be this: If I reached out a hand, a hand would reach back. I could ask for help, and help would arrive. It was as simple and as scary as that.

I had something concrete—an actual occurrence with significance assigned. *Okay, God,* I said to myself—*if that is your real name—I'll let you in a little.* "'Hope,'" said Emily Dickinson, "is the thing with feathers."[3]

A million questions and fears bubbled in a tremendous roiling pit of doubt. Beneath the churning was a void—a scary, novel stillness. But I sensed that the void was a temporary state, and I drove back home through that bright, sunlit afternoon with a willingness to believe that maybe, just maybe, grace was at work in my life, and that despite the hollowness I felt right then, something would flood in to fill that empty space.

2

⁂

THE POSITIVE SOUND

The mystery of grace is hard to comprehend and even harder to believe we deserve. But grace need never be earned, only received. As versatile as duct tape, as useful as helping hands, and as invigorating as a blast of fresh air, when the Holy Spirit wings in to ease the way, doing for us what we cannot—or will not—do for ourselves, that's grace. Grace is God's wild card. Devotion says, "Deal me in."

I wasn't looking for God's grace, explicitly, at first. In fact, given my rebellion against the church in which I was raised, I welcomed God in my life about as eagerly as I'd welcome an alien abduction or a tax audit. But then I was, as a friend put it, hit with the brick of salvation.

"I found Jesus," goes the old joke. "He was behind the couch." I, however, found him someplace equally unlikely—at the bottom of a tarry pit of despair.

Religious awakening, or reawakening, may coincide with recovering from addiction or a need to connect after the lonely agony of loss. For me, it stemmed from the desire to stay alive on this planet we call Earth, to stop maybe—for once—shredding myself with the lash of self-recrimination. I had gotten to a place near the middle of my life where I hated myself even more than usual—my inner voice saying louder than ever: *Failure. Fraud. Damaged goods. Everything is pointless.*

I have never viewed depression as a symptom of spiritual crisis. Diverting focus from the physiological element, which runs generations-deep in my family, seemed downright dangerous. But once I was properly medicated and back to functioning at a passable level, I realized that beneath the pain and aimlessness was a deep, oozing morass of cynicism and bitterness. The few beliefs I had were almost entirely negative: life is random, security is fleeting, and you're all alone in this world, so you'd better prepare for the worst. If there was something "bigger" out there, it was probably an Acme safe whistling through the air, sure to crush me flat.

Grace? Mercy? Miracles? The stuff of magical thinking.

Viewing life this way made sense to someone used to the emotional trap door beneath her opening up, sometimes when she least expected it, but I came to suspect that my cynicism might be part of the problem too. Where did faith fit into this? Anywhere?

My family of seven—two parents; one son and three daughters, each born about a year apart; and me, the caboose kid, five years later—wove in and out of religious observance in the Presbyterian church.

My father's career in the rut of corporate middle management had the family moving from Pennsylvania to Sweden, to Pennsylvania again (two different towns), then to Michigan, and finally, exhaustedly, to New Jersey. These moves, and the culture shock that accompanied each one, erased any sense of through-line in the family narrative. We were the Nowhereland Clan, rootless, socially awkward, perpetually bewildered. Even today, when someone asks me where I'm from, I have to pause as if it were a trick question.

My mother was raised with her sickly younger brother, Harvey, in their grandparents' Baltimore row house. She was brought up under a punishing strain of Norwegian Lutheranism, the sole purpose—or soul purpose—of which seemed to be responding to countless orders to prove yourself worthy of God. This left my mother gritting her teeth to follow rules her whole life while gasping for any sense of self-worth.

My father, the eldest son in a family of six kids raised by their widowed schoolteacher mother in Gibsonburg, Ohio, spent his childhood in the Methodist church. Devout advocates of observing the Sabbath, the Methodist elders made sure that not working on the weekend was drilled into my father, his two brothers, and three sisters, and they spent their off days riding to and from weekend retreats. He was born for the harness: a driven student, he shipped off to Harvard on scholarship, was drafted into Korea, then married my mother, fathered us, and powered through, short-fused as the demands kept their chokehold. Strangulation by necktie, all the way through to retirement.

My parents' religious upbringings cultivated in them a staunch work ethic coupled with an ingrained sense of shortcoming: a perfect combo-pack prescription for my future religious desertion. When they married, they left their churches and settled in the local Presbyterian congregation, full of young parents who socialized on weekends. Bridge club on Saturday night, early service on Sunday morning.

The experience of church—of worship—resides at the deepest core of my early memories. The waxy old linoleum in the Sunday school hallway, walls lined with felt banners of doves and olive branches. During services, I'd fidget next to my mother in the pew, doodling on my program with the tiny pencil tucked next to the offering envelopes, until the organ started up—a holy roaring from the pipes so mighty, you could feel it in your guts. We'd stand, eyes tilted down toward our hymnals, and sing, pray, then sing some more. I remember the shyness I'd feel, a little girl in a markdown Penney's Sunday dress and patent leather shoes, hiding behind my mother's leg as she turned to the people all around us to shake hands.

Peace be with you.

And also with you.

After school, my sisters would take me to Bible study. Mrs. Dernley, in her book-lined family room, would challenge us to recite bits of Scripture—*I am the resurrection and the life*—and for every correct recitation, we were rewarded with candy. As I memorized the Bible at night in the yellow bedroom I shared with my next-oldest sister, Kelly, I'd remember the crinkle of a plastic wrapper, the tartness of a lemon candy on my tongue like the communion host.

I didn't have a distinct sense of God, no feeling of divine presence around me, though I wanted to believe God was real. Mostly I was in it for the approval. For me, faith was a performance. I attended Sunday school with a thirsting heart, not so much because I was devoted to Jesus, but because I wanted my family to notice. I wanted to be loved.

By the time we moved to New Jersey, I was twelve, most of my siblings were out of the house, and my mom was wrung out. My parents greyed and tired, inertia took over, and faith fell to the way-side. My dad, who liked nothing more than puttering away a Sunday, didn't seem to miss church. He'd spend his day organizing the work-bench in the garage, recaning a chair, fixing a broken bike chain. The sacrament of shopcraft. My mother retreated to one of two spots—either curling up in the corner of our old, sagging, brown-striped couch, where she'd watch television until she fell asleep during the eleven o'clock news, or leaning on the sill of the kitchen sink, smok-ing mentholated Carltons and staring out the window while she ignored the dishes. And the laundry. And the cat, whose food some-times putrefied with maggots wriggling under the rim of the dish. The Church of Whatever. I didn't see it as troubling. The messiness inched forward by attrition, and it was normal . . . for us. It was just Mom being Mom.

My mother kept her faith in her humor, though. At the local flea market, she bought a goofy-looking stuffed grizzly that she named Gladly the Cross-Eyed Bear, a pun on the hymn "Gladly the Cross I'd Bear," and she'd laugh whenever I recited the punch line to my favorite joke about Christ on the cross: "Peter . . . I can see your house from here!" But I'd never again hear her fine voice singing "Angels We Have Heard on High" or "What Wondrous Love Is This."

I was happy to escape Sunday school and, as a teenager, I had no interest in joining a church youth group like my sisters. I had less than no interest in ministry, like my oldest sister, Barbara, who started seminary the same year I started high school. The entirety of my church experience left me with little more than the resolution that Sunday mornings are better spent sleeping in, and the belief through observation that faith can't conquer apathy.

My mother was always a fan of books and performance. She could snap out of her funk when culture called. She accidentally radicalized me by taking me to see Allen Ginsberg at William Paterson University when I was seventeen. As he recited and sang his poetry, he laid out my future in the rhythm of a contemplative Hebrew chant mixed with a battle cry: "I saw the best minds of my generation destroyed by madness . . ."[1] Hippie counterculture wasn't my movement, it wasn't my *bag*, but the ferocious drive of his words shook me awake. After that, creative expression was my religion, my salvation, my altar of worship. The first safe harbor for a weird kid is art.

Church, then, became for me a bunch of uptight, humorless people who never got laid. Art—the righteous screams of underground poets, the machine-gun syncopation of punk rock drums—was something I could believe in. Music was sacred. Words were sacred. Spare me the Bible and give me *The Bell Jar.*

When I fell into a depression so severe I dropped out of high school, I retreated to my room in our cookie-cutter housing development split-level, angry and alone, and I took my raging art with me into the isolation chamber. When all you have is a hammer, everything looks like a nail. *Bang, bang,* there I was: Thor of Suburbia.

I took my teenage rage to the streets of New York City, marching down Sixth Avenue against traffic in a protest against the nuclear arms race. I ended up getting arrested with my high school friend Jeanette. We were cuffed, loaded into a paddy wagon, and brought to central booking in lower Manhattan, otherwise known as the Tombs. Jeanette and I were illegally strip-searched and held overnight, apart from the rest of our group, who were all adults, and we shivered in a juvie cell with a couple of underage prostitutes who had been brought in as part of a roundup. We never heard our Miranda rights or got to make a phone call. The charges against us were dropped when civil rights activist William Kunstler showed up in the courtroom, citing freedom of assembly, freedom of speech, and police malfeasance. But

I never forgot the feeling of the cold, steel bunk under my thighs, and the callous female cops' voices as they instructed me to strip down and bend forward.

I moved to the East Village when I was eighteen and found a comfortable spot in the margins, discovering, with no surprise, that the "least of these" were the people I liked the most—the self-exiled punk kids, the runaways, the radical squatters, the spare-changers on Saint Marks Place, the lunatic touring musicians, and the dropouts like me, our macerated hearts beating fiercely under black leather jackets. I came to view organized religion as the ultimate con, a sexist, backward means of maintaining the status quo. Music and art were the only things that reached beyond that scaly cynicism and left me in awe. When I saw Karen Finley recite her psalmlike poem "The Black Sheep," my mind was blown. I stood at the side of the stage, sobbing as she read:

> *We are members of the*
> *Black Sheep family—*
> *We are sheep with no shepherd—*
> *We are sheep with no straight and narrow*
> *We are sheep with no meadow*
> *We are sheep who take the dangerous*
> *pathway thru the mountain range*
> *to get to the other side of our soul.*[2]

Everyone around me—every punk, freak, tweaker, junkie, poet, painter, and loser—was trying to express the inexpressible. For a gang of underachievers, we sure produced a lot: poetry readings, charity fund-raisers, chapbooks, fanzines, records, xeroxed posters and flyers, and Krylon-sprayed statements that defaced public property. Some of us were small-time drug dealers; most of us sweated it out waitressing, working minimum-wage retail, and tending bar. A small number of us, myself included, worked to the smoky beat in red-light district clubs. We kept that part of ourselves well hidden, knowing how harshly we'd be judged and how hard it would be to examine our choices, like our bruises, in the broad light of day. We slid our insecurities under a veil of daring, and we kept our fear obscured under dim nightclub lighting laced with curling wisps of cigarette smoke. Whether we worked buttering up customers waiting tables in a café or flattering lonely men in grungy dives, we told the truth on our own time.

A wise writer said that "anger is sad's bodyguard." Through our art, or attempts at it, we reached past the rage, clinging to each other as we revealed our vulnerable selves to the world: we were limpets in alligator suits.

But that was years ago, when working on the edge seemed worth the risk, and the fire of youthful outrage could singe away a dark night of the soul. That's not an approach that weathers well; eventually you realize that cockiness, rebel anger, and fangirl adrenaline alone won't keep you going.

When my life got complicated by, you know, life—when I had been married awhile, when my responsibilities mounted, when people I knew started getting sick or slipping off the rails, and when my own hopes and dreams crashed—I needed stronger medicine. Throughout my adulthood, I had tried everything: therapy, medication, meditation. Everything except God.

I cry easily. I cry over friends' weddings, sick children, cute dogs, birthday cards, sad songs, and sonogram photos where the baby is but a hopeful little blob bobbing in a black sea of womb. I'm often embarrassed at how thin the wall is between a neutral state of mind and open weeping, but within the waterworks is a pinprick of hope: I know that residing in me is a willingness to be moved, even when stubborn emotional resistance shows up to block the proceedings.

A few years ago, network cable stations featured a commercial for a compilation of Christian praise music. It was on the air constantly, the song titles scrolling over stock nature images—sunsets, breaking waves, mighty snowcapped peaks breaking through the clouds. Then, over the snippet of "Place in This World" by Michael W. Smith, there was footage of a concert audience. Hands were raised, people of all ages swayed back and forth in the packed arena, the crowd dotted with the tiny lights of cell phones held up like lighters. The camera took a tight shot of a young woman, her dark hair pulled back, a few loose tendrils pasted by sweat to her damp forehead. Her eyes were closed, tears streaming, her palms held up as she rocked back and forth to the lyrics—something about roaming through the night to find a place in this world.

I had the strongest urge to mock this woman out loud. The sight of her annoyed me. *Look at that kook. She's doing that in public! Doesn't she care how she looks to other people?* It didn't take long to identify the hot, prickly feeling that fanned out from the center of my chest: I was jealous. I wanted what she had. Of course she didn't care how she looked. She had gone to another place. Someplace pure, where self-consciousness couldn't reach. The expression on her face was unmistakable: Surrender. Bliss.

Soon after that, weeping to the radio became standard practice, especially in the car. I would turn on the local Christian station and cry and cry. My husband, whenever he got behind the wheel, would give me the side-eye as he turned the ignition and the radio would come on to some DJ letting us know we were listening to "the *positive* sound. The sound of life."

I couldn't help it. I'd start out looking for something new and catchy to listen to; then a song would strike me at a certain angle, hitting something located so powerfully in my heart that it became part of me, a steady pulse thrumming through every longing moment: *I want to believe, I want to believe, I want to believe.* The simplest lyric could set me off. The Holy Spirit moved, it seemed, through my tear ducts.

I wanted to find God, but I couldn't even find my car keys most of the time. And I didn't have the freedom, or the energy, to make any kind of pilgrimage. On a good day, I could manage a trip to the grocery store. With no option for boundless seeking, could I find what I needed spiritually closer to home, with what few free hours I could carve out? Could something simple, some kind of kitchen-sink enlightenment, be within reach?

I started touring Presbyterian churches. New York City, with its variety, vitality, and busy churn that matches my own internal rhythm, has always been my holy ground, so I searched within its limits. I went to famous, fashionable, Upper West Side churches, such as Redeemer, that catered to the professional class, and I went to historic churches, such as First Presbyterian in the Village, where the lead pastor, Jon Walton, hosted and sanctified gay marriages long before the presbytery voted to allow congregations to perform them, even though he risked facing censure—Christian conscience with "come at me, bro" swagger. I went to Resurrection in Williamsburg (hyped in the *New York Times* style pages with the regrettable headline "A Congregation in Skinny Jeans"), where a trio played a rockabilly version of "Just a Closer Walk with Thee" with a walking bass line plunked out on stand-up. The pastor, a fantastic guy named Vito Aiuto, who wore dad cardigans, served communion with an option of nonalcoholic wine and gluten-free bread. I knew what I wanted: a church with women on its pastoral staff, because I believe in female leadership in all arenas, and the church had to be affirming—welcoming gay, lesbian, and trans people without the "love the sinner, hate the sin" equivocation—because I couldn't do "God accepts everyone" with an asterisk. I sampled churches big and small, radical and traditional, on huge avenues and quiet side streets, looking for the best fit, looking, more than anything, for a place that felt like home. A place that felt just right. I was Goldilocks with a God-shaped hole.

I once asked Barbara, My Sister the Minister, how she got the call to ministry.

"When I was little," she said, "I had night terrors, so Mom would soothe me by saying that God watched over me and that everything would be okay. After that, I had a very real sense of God. He was just there. Always." She felt the presence of God around her as if she were wrapped in a warm blanket.

That, right there, was the difference between me and what I thought of as a true believer. I had a suspicion, an inkling, that there was something out there, something divine and otherworldly, that I could call God. But that feeling came and went—as a concept, not a physical sensation.

I decided that my doubt wasn't a disqualifier. Pascal's Wager, an argument devised by the seventeenth-century French philosopher and physicist Blaise Pascal, posits that it is in one's own best interest to behave as if God exists, since the advantages of belief outweigh any advantage of disbelief. I could choose to fully believe. I could act "as if."

My faith wasn't going to be a gift I would greet with surprise and wonder; it would be a decision, a commitment I would see through. At the very least it gave me something to do while I tried to figure out how to save my own skin. Pascal's Wager was a way back from the brink.

Even if Jesus Christ weren't real, living "as if" might drastically change things for the better. I wanted to do more than set things right inside myself; I also wanted to help reclaim the word *Christian*, which, like reclaiming the words *patriot* and *freedom-loving*, meant reeling things back in a more inclusion-based direction. My spiritual itch wasn't just personal. It was also political. Devotion can come with an edge of uprising, and sometimes the most rebellious thing you can do is to stare in the face of doubt and say yes anyway.

As though to reinforce this thinking, Scott Black Johnston, the preacher at the next church I attended—Fifth Avenue Presbyterian, a big, elegant affair right across the street from Gucci—delivered a sermon on the divinity of crabbiness, of feeling out of sorts, even out of sync, with God. Throughout his sermon, he emphasized that you don't have to be perfect, or in a good mood, or even passably presentable, to be with God or be loved by God. You can bring your doubts. You can show up in pieces. Doubt and vulnerability aren't flaws; they are characteristics central to our identities that God abides, unconditionally. Uncertainty is a feature, not a bug.

This notion that I am loved—that we are all loved, no matter what—felt so unfamiliar to me that it was almost threatening. Because it seemed too good to be true. Because it meant that all my days and months and years of self-loathing and regret represented time wasted, hours that could never be recaptured. There's no extra-credit assignment to boost your grade in God's eyes. No gold star to earn. Nothing I could produce to better secure my position.

For a New Yorker by choice, driven and defined by what I have—or too often, haven't—accomplished, this was anathema. New York is the Cathedral of Win. You fight to keep your place. There's no "done deal" here. My self-worth spikes and dips like an index fund, rising and falling in line with how I'm perceived. Who am I without my accomplishments or the sum of my failures? Who are we all?

If you told me I could meet Jesus, I'd try to lose ten pounds first—so God's love as a come-as-you-are proposition seemed impossible. But in that huge, exquisite church on Fifth Avenue, I could almost wrap my arms around the idea.

Redeemer, on the Upper West Side, was too conservative for my comfort, but I appreciated the clear intellect and shrewd humor of the sermon by the lead pastor, David Kim, and sought him out for conversation. In his midtown office, Reverend Kim told me how, in his twenties, he had gone from being a microbiology major at Penn to a Princeton Theological Seminary student. We talked a bit about the break between the secular world and faith: How, I asked, do you gracefully, diplomatically, explain your belief? What would you tell people is the singular defining element of Christianity if they asked you "Why Jesus?" I was fishing for his pitch, basically, simultaneously seeking a way in and an excuse to punt.

"The defining element of Christianity doesn't lie so much in the story of Christ's birth," Reverend Kim said, "but in the miracle of the resurrection. The message at the heart of Christ's crucifixion and his rise from the tomb is this: pain isn't the end of the story."

Pain isn't the end of the story.

My toughened, tired heart was pierced. Reverend Kim already knew I wasn't destined to join his congregation, so a personally tailored sales proposal wouldn't work. Yet here he was, telling me something I desperately needed to hear, when everything, for so long, had seemed so raw and wounding and impossible. Pain isn't the end of the story. This God was the God of second chances, of grace, of ample opportunity for a divine do-over.

Reverend Kim and the church where he worked didn't have to be 100 percent in line with my views to provide meaningful ministry. While the mainstream never seemed safe to me and I found refuge in the far corners, I could always use the reminder that there is goodness at the center too. As Malcolm Boyd, the pioneering gay Episcopalian said, "Real answers need to be found in dialogue and interaction and, yes, our shared human condition. This means being open to one another instead of simply fighting to maintain a prescribed position."[3]

Touring different congregations and seeking a place that felt progressive and inclusive had a galvanizing effect, bringing together two parts of me I thought might never meet: devotion and ferocity. I could be both a lover *and* a fighter. I found myself feeling more receptive to making a boon companion of mystery, to being enchanted, or even rescued, by forces I couldn't quite comprehend.

I'd found out through a random web search that Michael W. Smith, of "Place in This World" fame, was playing at Carnegie Hall. By the time I checked, there were only two seats left, way up in the nosebleed section, each under thirty dollars.

When I got to Carnegie Hall, I realized that *nosebleed section* did not describe these seats. *Panic attack section* would have been more accurate. As a lifelong acrophobe, the climb up three, then four, then—*gulp*—five flights of stairs freaked me out. By the time I found my seat, with a view straight down a couple hundred feet, I was shaking, cold liquid lightning shooting down my legs. My knees started to buckle.

I turned around and went back downstairs. I spent the first half of the show wandering the hallway, looking at the framed autographed headshots of Marian Anderson, George Gershwin, and Igor Stravinsky while I listened through the closed doors. I'd come all this way, and fear was holding me back. How telling.

I ginned up my nerve after intermission. I had to see Smith play "Place in This World." Had to. I consulted the program—it was the song coming up next. My heart racing, palms slippery, I edged my way into my seat, avoiding looking down. I prayed for strength; I prayed for Klonopin. I held on to the railing with one hand and my armrest with the other.

Finally, Smith started "Place in This World," but after two hours of performing, his voice was fatigued, cracking on the high notes. I had hoped to make a powerful connection to the song that had stamped my passport on this journey, but it didn't happen. The peak moment that wasn't.

Then, out of the darkness, came the lowing of a viola, followed by a few notes on the piano and the choir singing "Alleluia." Carnegie Hall took on that shimmer where you sense some strange musical alchemy taking place. Tears prickled up in the corners of my eyes. Everyone started singing along with "Agnus Dei." The lyrics passed by me in pieces: "holy, holy . . . Lord God almighty . . . worthy is the Lamb . . . Amen."

I didn't know the words, so I could only listen. In the midst of the lyrics rose a song above the song, pulling everyone along the same current. There was an animating presence there, something bigger than all of us, mysterious but familiar too.

I clung with one hand to that armrest, vibrating from a palm-dampening convergence of fright, exhilaration, and hope. We were all very much in this moment, each one of us, from the big-ticket Holy Rollers in the orchestra section all the way up to me, the chicken-hearted weeper in the cheap seats. In this city of countless cathedrals, this was the closest I'd ever felt to God, and to New York. Studies show that the church is dying, but then, people are always saying that New York is dying, too, and yet here we all were, cramped, broken, and magnificently alive as ever.

I kept swiping my eyes with the same mangled tissue, buoyed by the affirmation that the fangirl rush is a holy thing indeed. The tears felt baptismal, as if the parched, fallow field of me were being watered. Refreshed.

When it comes to the whole Christianity package, doubt may be my constant companion, but in that moment, I was certain that the Holy Spirit was as present in Carnegie Hall as in any designated house of worship. I was drawn in by an undeniable sense of relief and belonging. My place in this world—our place—was here, now, forging a covenant of sound. For it was the sound that brought us together, the black sheep and the holy lambs, every one of us straining to hang on. Straining to make that connection. Straining to hear that divine chord.

3

BAD CHRISTIANS AND
OTHER GOOD PEOPLE

The sign on the church basement wall said, "The difference between something being an ordeal and an adventure depends on your perspective." The edges of the paper were worn, the sign smeared with what looked like fingerprints of motor oil. I wondered if it had been stolen from a mechanic's shop.

Some of us are, for reasons both admirable and repellent, always looking for a guarantee: that we won't get hurt, that the outcome will be what was forecasted, that there are no hidden commitment clauses. Call us "proof junkies," addicted to the illusion of certainty and control. We like to think we call the shots. Ha! More often, our lives are illustrations of the saying "If you want to make God laugh, tell him your plans."

Staring blankly at the grease-monkey gospel as I waited for the recovery group meeting to begin, I began to suspect that, quite apart from the physiological makeup of my own faulty brain chemistry, this control thing might be part of the problem.

I didn't need an intervention from sweet, blond-haired, Kenny-Loggins-look-alike Jesus, the washer-of-feet and walker-on-water. I needed Dumpster-fire Jesus. Forget the crown of thorns, buddy. Put on a hazmat suit instead.

Like Ghandi, I liked Christianity but not Christians. Still, Christ was calling to me. I was already Team Jesus by the rite of baptism, and with that bald eagle, he'd sent me something as close to a miracle as I'd ever seen. Wasn't seeing what else God had in store the polite thing to do?

Christianity offered a laundry list of things I found unappealing or downright unacceptable. I was turned off by terms like *cafeteria Christians*, which is meant to deride those who dare to personalize how they receive God's Word by picking and choosing from the Bible to suit their needs (as opposed to buying into a wholly articulated and prescribed theological line). This judgment seemed so small and mean to me—and very telling, given how the school cafeteria looms large in our collective memory as a site of social torment. Cliques and clucking tongues should be the stuff of nightmares and John Hughes movies, not the church. Aren't we all just trying to find a seat at a friendly table?

People who only show up at church for Christmas and Easter are dismissed as *Creasters*. (What would they call those of us who hadn't shown up for, oh, twenty-five years? *Defectors? Failures?*) It reminded me of the episode of *The Big Bang Theory* in which Sheldon and Amy discuss God in their pedantic, eggheaded way: "I don't object to the concept of a deity," Amy says, "but I'm baffled by the notion of one that takes attendance."[1]

Who needs a faith that comes with its own snide litany of ways that people fall short of some vaunted ideal? As hospitality tactics go, the messaging could use a bit of refinement. *Welcome to church: You're doing it wrong.*

Godsplaining—the strict insistence on theological purity and consistency in worship—didn't go over well with me, a person who didn't want to go to church because not only did I mistrust authority, but also Sunday services competed with brunch. I didn't need to be beaten back with a rigid set of standards. I wasn't trying to be the president of Jesus. I was just trying to survive.

I remembered my uncle Harvey delivering a eulogy years ago. Harvey was an agnostic who kept his beliefs close to the vest—a good guy, if not a godly guy. In his trim Baltimore summer seersucker, he stood at the podium and said, "Some people go to church on Sunday and spend the whole time thinking about fishing; some people go fishing on Sundays and spend the whole time thinking about God." That sounded about right to me. Isn't the connection more important than the location?

The writer Roxane Gay liberated me, or at least nudged me a little further over the church threshold, with the introduction to her book *Bad Feminist*: "I'd rather be a bad feminist than no feminist at all," she wrote. "I embrace the label of bad feminist because I am human. I am messy. I'm not trying to be an example. I am not trying to be perfect. I am not trying to say I have all the answers. I am not trying to say I'm right. I am just trying—trying to support what I believe in, trying to do some good in this world."[2]

If she could be a Bad Feminist, I could be a Bad Christian. Better that than no Christian at all. I was bitter, suspicious, disallowing, and petrified, but I was also ready for God's next step for me, however it might appear. A swirl cone of half-aging hipster crunch, half-gooey, pliant vanilla.

I didn't have to pledge to join a particular congregation, and I didn't have to get it right the first time, or ever. If a church, or a pastor, had any shiny sliver of hope or encouragement to offer me, I could take it, even if we weren't spiritual soul mates. When it came to deliverance, I'd put it together piece by piece. The crazy quilt of salvation.

When I started to sweat, thinking I'd picked the *worst possible* spiritual endeavor for my authority-averse, control-freaky self, I'd walk through the church doors remembering what my friend Jenne said to me: "Church is a hospital for sinners, not a gallery for saints."

After a year of faithful attendance, I graduated from my group therapy program. At least I knew I could show up regularly for something. My goal after I emerged was threefold: first to stay alive, then to feel grounded, and then to find something to give in return for the gift of survival.

I needed a new group. A squad, if you will. I'm from a big family—I like being part of the gang. By now, I had enough oversight of my depression to know that seeing people I loved struggling with addiction to drugs and alcohol was a big factor. Friends appeared to let me know there were others, just like me, who could help. My buddy Amanda calls it "the struggle bus." I was ready to board.

There is no situation in your life made more difficult by looking straight at it, and I had to admit that I was being made crazy by my futile attempts at rescuing others. I have flushed friends' pre-scription speed down toilets, only to have them steal more from another friend's medicine cabinet. I have loaned out money that went straight up someone's nose, never to be seen again. Then a friend checked herself into an eight-thousand-dollar-a-week detox center in Connecticut, only to emerge and get drunk on a seven-dollar six-pack of Budweiser that night. She went to work hungover and was immediately fired. Her employer had paid for her stint in rehab. I didn't know what to say to her, or how best to support her. I was in way over my head, and I was literally making myself sick with worry.

I'm not much of a drinker. When I was in high school, I spent a few nights pounding Midori on the rocks in the cocktail lounge at the local Holiday Inn, listening to an awful cover band play 1970s metal power ballads, but I spun away the drunk lying atop the black-and-white checkerboard polyblend comforter on my twin bed without my parents catching on. I didn't toss my cookies, but I came so close that if I catch a whiff of melon-scented body lotion even today, I gag. When my husband and I lived in military quarters on West Point, a houseguest gave us a hostess gift of an elegant metal-lic rose magnum of champagne worth as much as we earned in a week—but instead of guzzling it, I regifted the bottle, and I think it got left in the corner of a loft in Williamsburg. I have my vices, but drink and drugs don't tempt me. I consider this more a matter of luck than willpower.

But just because you're sober doesn't mean you're not sick. If someone I love is high or drunk or in a mess because of one state of intoxication or another, I will wade into the scene thinking I'm Aquaman when I'm really a myopic dolt with a leaky raft. Not only was I punching above my weight class by trying to navigate a territory I knew nothing about—addiction—but I was getting in the way of desperate people figuring things out for themselves. I needed to learn that addicts and alcoholics have to tend to the parts of themselves that nothing else can fix—not a drink, not a drug, not a relationship, not an accomplishment. Not even you.

Hanging with this welcoming, sage, and annoyingly patient group of people who, like me, loved the addicted and afflicted, I kept running into the expression "Let go and let God," which made me want to run the other way. It sounded so joyfully subservient, almost culty. The exact thing I despise—devotion as drug of choice. As my friend Mary says, "Happy-clappy Jesus is just dope with a beard and a walking stick." Let go? Why? And let God do *what*?

Then a tall, curvy biker chick named Frannie showed me the light. In Frannie's back pocket, dangling from a silver chain, she carried a black leather Harley-Davidson wallet embossed with the words *Screw housework, let's ride*. She was also a rabid couponer, which worked for me. Frannie knew what the deal was *and* where the deals were. With a single silver braid of hair dangling all the way down to her belt loops, she was a tough but practical customer; and I like that in a gal. God bless a woman who's got *stories*.

One day, Frannie recited a version of the classic Christian poem "Footprints," which can be found on everything from framed plaques to bookmarks to dish towels, describing a walk along the sand with God by your side, the two of you making footprints as you go. At some point during the walk, there is only one set of footprints in the sand, and the verse describes the tender care of the Lord thusly: The Lord will never leave you. When you feared that seeing only one set of footprints in the sand meant that God had left you, no! There was only one set of footprints in the sand because—cue the Kleenex—*God had carried you!*

Except in Frannie's version, instead of the poem ending with one set of footprints in the sand, it ended with a set of footprints in the sand alongside a long, deep trench, because God had to drag you.

She understood how "Let go and let God" could sound sappy and resigned—and to me, resignation was the least attractive proposition ever. I hadn't yet learned the difference between resigning, which is among the weakest acts, and surrendering, which is among the most powerful. Resignation means giving up, whereas surrender means giving over. Surrender is admitting that there are other hands at work. Frannie suggested that instead of "Let go and let God," we should "Let go or get dragged," which was a revelation.

I finally got it. If you can get me to laugh, you can get me to listen.

Mostly Frannie encouraged me to understand the value of being patient with myself while everything still sucks, and turning over to God the trials I couldn't solve, weather, or shift on my own. I learned you don't have to show up in great shape to get started; that, she informed me, made about as much sense as cleaning before the maid came. You show up broken and mushed up against the windshield. You start right where you are, at a slow, pathetic, bitter, and neurotic crawl. The price of admission was nothing more than your own willingness to be transformed, against all logic, against all evidence to the contrary.

Those of us who have been duking it out on our own have a hard time with surrender. We're not used to help, and we're not used to trust. Instead we regard as immutable our grinding resignation that everything falls on us to tolerate, spur forward, or fix. Call us "hard as nails" and we take it as a compliment.

Can people like me unpeel one grippy monkey paw from things, for even a few seconds? Could I hold tight to the idea that maybe God's path for me was better than my own best thinking, which, I was finally willing to face, had already brought me to the brink far too many times? Hell, my best thinking had almost led me to jump off a bridge.

The late author Robert M. Pirsig wrote, "The place to improve the world is first in one's own heart and head and hands, and then work outward from there."[3] So many of us resist the truth that self-care is not self-indulgence, but it is a fact that you cannot pour from an empty cup. Or a shattered one.

I have always relied on my inner resources, but ever so slowly, these friends got me to understand that I was, fortunately or unfortunately, only human, and there were other resources available. Higher resources. I could stand back when something troubled me and say, *You know what? I can't take this.*

God, you take it.

Frannie's penetration of the cement form called my skull led to the first time I acknowledged that God might move through other people to reach me. It is said, "Don't ask for signs and then ignore the signs." And don't ignore the people who show up right when you admit you need someone. Just then, about all I could do was half-assed devotion with a few shots of sarcasm and vinegar, and Frannie seemed to think that was pretty great. Progress not perfection, she'd remind me. I'd roll my eyes.

As much as I wondered why God had never seemed to pick up when I called, or answer the prayers I sent up—prioritized and detailed to my exacting specifications—Frannie reminded me that prayers weren't wish lists and that I was praying to God, not Santa Claus. She also reminded me that this was the God of wonders both large and small—not only of love and kindness and reconstruction, but also periwinkles, Dolly Parton, zip-front hoodies, and Taco Tuesday. Frannie would bonk me in the snout with various directives that I hated, such as "Lighten up" or "Easy does it."

I didn't have to give anyone anything; I could just be the grateful recipient of their love and support. That was hard for me, almost as hard as taking leave of reason and letting other forces take over. *There are a million reasons why this can't possibly work,* I told myself. But I kept palling around with this crew, with their bad jokes and bitter coffee, despite my resistance, and I started to see a little lavender glow of dawn out the corner of my eye. That's the difference between skepticism and pessimism: skeptics question the miracle; pessimists miss the miracle entirely.

For my religious rebirth, I'd wanted a controlled, sterile environment, or at least a set itinerary or a guarantee of redemption (whatever that meant).

But a quick consultation with your nearest Bible shows that spiritual growth looks like that exactly never. Theologian Frederick Buechner said that "a Christian is one who is on the way, though not necessarily very far along it, and who has at least some dim and half-baked idea of whom to thank."[4] Sometimes the ordeal *is* the adventure, and you're the best journeyman you can be when you show up exactly the way you are: half-baked, half-crazy, on your way.

4

HOLY DAY

Every October, the animatronic life-size mummy takes his place of honor on my front porch. By then, I'm already intoxicated by the sensory delights of autumn: The smell of burning leaves. A sliver of horned harvest moon obscured in the night sky by scuttering platinum-edged clouds. Racks of horrifying costumes—zombies, witches, monsters—scaring the crap out of kids in the local shops. Halloween is the perfect holiday for depressed people because no one asks you to be cheerful.

For the grown-up Goths, freaks, weirdos, and other miscellaneous self-identified creeps I call my tribe, this, not Christmas, is "the most wonderful time of the year." I thrill at rows of Styrofoam headstones askew on a lawn, skeleton hands reaching from under the lid of an ersatz coffin. I admire the holiday's sly paradox. Halloween allows us to wear death lightly.

By my own definition, a Goth is someone who likes gloomy, macabre music, culture, and clothing; someone whose romantic, rebel heart is barbed wire–bound by a wry sense of irony about doom, religion, the afterlife, and the underworld. If you've ever seen someone walking around in, say, July, dressed in a way that makes you want to call out, "Hey, freak! Halloween is over!" *C'est un* Goth.

Halloween is a misfit's high holy day, but I didn't comprehend the sacred aspects of Halloween until I'd celebrated it as a baby Goth, all of sixteen years old, in a gay neighborhood. As a questioning teen, the trip to the Greenwich Village Halloween Parade was a pilgrimage of incalculable personal value. The event illustrated that the ritual of dressing up—of choosing an alternate persona—can be the quickest route to self-affirmation. Show me a young man in a woman's costume, and, as often as not, I see someone hiding in plain sight. Show me a girl entranced with Victorian mourning attire and other aesthetics of death, and I see someone who's trying to figure out life. By its own curious nature, Goth culture lent me a critical coping skill for weathering my own depression: if you're stuck in perpetual midnight, find beauty in the dark.

Goths, with their fixation on stylized morbidity, may seem to be tough customers at first glance of their black velvet capes and blood-red lips, but as Cole Porter sang, it ain't necessarily so. Once, during a photo shoot in an old graveyard when I was nineteen, I nearly fell into a partially sunken grave and shot clear out of my skin—thus proving that you can be both a Goth *and* a wuss.

When I was twenty-one, I moved from New York to San Francisco, seeking what is known in the recovery circles as "the geographic cure," hoping that I could distance myself from my problems by changing coasts. But the transition from the New York punk scene to the leather-and-chains Gothic corners of San Francisco not only failed to grant me a single inch of distance from my troubles but also presented me with the immeasurable sorrow of seeing my newfound brothers and sisters ravaged by disease and institutional indifference. If you think that participation in this death-as-high-camp culture would have inured me to seeing the reaper run his wrecking ball through our self-selected family at the height of the AIDS crisis, it didn't. If you think it can lessen the pain of grief that stalks me each Halloween that I live without them, it cannot. The epidemic is now framed as history, but I still live in that loss every day.

That Goth style exerts such a strong pull on LGBTQ people comes as no surprise. For many, the movie *The Hunger* acted as a gateway drug, making polymorphously perverse immortality appear gorgeous just as we were worried we wouldn't survive our own befuddling, isolated adolescences. The vampire is our ultimate relatable anti-hero: Dangerous desire. Limited hours of safe operation. Hiding in shadows. These are familiar themes that, for all their implied risk, are oddly comforting; this sinister subculture becomes, ironically, a safe space. The same can be said for the ghoul's paradise of Halloween, when the deathly becomes delightful, and what is terrifying becomes irresistible. You make a friend of danger. You hide, seek, and are sought, an identity pieced together through peekaboo. In his essay "Girl," beloved novelist Alexander Chee wrote about his first Halloween foray into female drag: "Sometimes you don't know who you are until you put on a mask."[1]

With my boundless affection for darkness and the cobwebby margins, it has been disorienting to find that—like Linus waiting in the patch for the Great Pumpkin—I believe, with this faith of surprisingly Jesus-y shape. I considered, at first, trying to be a cut-and-dried mainline Bible-thumper, but I love all that spooky, mystical woo-woo too much.

During my church hunt, I'd heard a lot of good things about a certain Presbyterian church in Manhattan, so I showed up at their congregation's uptown location feeling doubtful, unsure of the value of the endeavor and wondering if I'd fit in. According to the Pew Research Group, 55 percent of people pray daily, including 44 percent of the nonreligious.[2] That morning, I had only one explicit prayer: "Make it obvious, Lord." If I was meant to keep on with this Christianity thing, I asked, please show me a sign. Not, like, a vague "feather on the wind" kind of sign. Something eagle-level obvious. Something even a bonehead like me couldn't ignore.

At this church, a certain intelligence was assumed. Their brochures read "Skeptics welcome." I should have felt at home there, but I didn't. Everyone was so well-dressed. The sermon—delivered by an all-male pastoral staff—reminded me of a TED talk. I kept scanning the pews, feeling myself rapidly curdling into Bill Maher. Turning fully around, I looked at the very last row. Sitting in the aisle seat was an older gentleman with shaggy dyed black hair, white Gucci slip-ons, and clothes that could best be described as "Goth golfer casual."

I squinted. *No. Nope. Can't be.* I had to bite my lips to keep from laughing.

Alice Cooper is in this church.

Alice Cooper is in this church.

Having spent most of my miserable teenage years under the headphones, walled off from the world with music as my lone sanctuary, Cooper's *Welcome to My Nightmare* album was one of my favorites. Didn't someone once say "Coincidence is God's way of remaining anonymous"? Short of a spectral visitation from Joey Ramone wearing vestments, I couldn't see how this could have been more obvious. That prayer? Asked and answered. And my church program? Autographed.

In the end, I learned that this particular church wasn't a good fit for me because it wasn't affirming. This was a problem, because if you took away all the parts of me that have been shaped by LGBTQ experiences, friends, relatives, colleagues, and culture, all that'd be left is peroxide and an underfunded SEP-IRA. As I embarked on my church-hunt, the greatest concern came from the queer corners— *Hold it just a minute there, Churchy McJesus*—which makes sense given how many LGBTQ people have been alienated, if not outright damaged, through a repressive religious upbringing. So many people have been traumatized by religion or religion-based prejudice that telling them "I'm praying for you" isn't an affirmation but a trigger. We are only now, as a country, outlawing gay conversion programs, many of which are church-based.

The dangled promise of God's love, and the threat of its removal, ceases to be incentive to stay put when you're exhausted from suffering abusive, rejecting, or exploitative people operating under the cover of the cross. But it's important to make the distinction that being abused, rejected, and disillusioned by a church is *not* the same as being abused or rejected by God, because by God's loving grace, such a thing is impossible. Everyone is chosen. Everyone is loved. Even if certain congregations run afoul of this truth. Emily Dickinson, patron saint poetess of many a Goth, said, "If your Nerve, deny you— / Go above your Nerve."[3] I'd adapt that to say, "If your church deny you, by all means, go above your church."

It came as a relief when my denomination, the Presbyterian Church (USA) voted to formally allow its churches to perform gay weddings, joining the Episcopalians, the Evangelical Lutheran Church in America, and the United Church of Christ. (Interestingly, a recent Pew study showing a declivitous slide in American Christianity found that 48 percent of LGBTQ Americans now identify as Christian.[4]) Now I can worship at several churches with ease in my heart, knowing that a huge swath of my social world, my band of misfits, would be welcome. My only regret is that AIDS took so many of them before they could behold this seismic shift.

Halloween (aka All Hallow's Eve) and the days that immediately follow, All Saints' and All Souls' Days—both on the Christian calendar—are said to be when the barrier between the dead and the living is at its thinnest, but I feel that divide evanescent at all times, connection passing back and forth as we move unawares. Even separated by death, the fallen lost ones and I, we are each other's light in the dark. Whenever I enter a church, their spirits go with me.

I had assumed that by returning to church, I'd have to cut Halloween from my list of sacred seasons, but I'm figuring out now that faith brings you closer to your true self, not further away. We can be devoted and not denatured. God loves us when we bring the weird.

Every November 2, I will remember my dearly departed—those hobgoblin activists who introduced me to the sacrament of mischief. Those lost boys and girls who helped me find myself. I will never disavow my shadowy past—Goth culture helped me make sense of my own darkness, to see the transformative beauty of elevating pain and sorrow to art. As is asked in one of the Sisters of Mercy's classic Goth dirges, "Would you carry the torch for me?" Always.

Together, Halloween, All Saints' Day, and All Souls' Day represent an exaltation of escape and revelry, as well as somber respect for death and those whom it has claimed—primitive rite and Christian tradition joining hands. I still love graveyards, rattling chains, black cats, and all manner of spooky things. And I adore the blessing of sacred serendipity—that you can discover yourself while pretending to be someone else. That you can pray for a guiding angel and God will send Alice Cooper. So let us rejoice in this glorious, ghoulish time when we honor all souls, all saints, what we reveal of our personal truth through artifice, and the ghosts of our former selves.[5]

5

BOX OF TERRORS

In the playroom in the damp, spider-dense basement of our second Pennsylvania house, there was a box inside of a box—a game
called Flower Lotto that we stored, with the Monopoly board and
the Uno deck, in a water-stained pine toy chest shoved against the
chipping stucco wall. The walls of the playroom were painted white,
the wood trim was a clownish cherry red, and the remnant carpet
over the cement floors was a royal blue, so the room felt frozen into
an ongoing Fourth of July celebration. The premise of the game was
simple: mix up the flowered pieces and match one pretty posy with
another—pansy with pansy, violet with violet, two cheerful daisies
paired and added to the pile.

For a gum-stuck-in-her-hair kid who never made her bed or got up for school on time, it was a perfect pastime—a game that whimsi-cally forced patience and organization.

All my life, I've wanted things to be easily sorted, but I had my cards tossed in the air early. It's been tough to make sense of things ever since.

Depression has a physiological component, but often, it also has an origin story called Trauma. The trauma story contains the possibility of a happy ending, but getting there sure can take awhile. The road to the destination we hope for—peace and comfort and a roomy, trusting heart—must be navigated with gentleness, and diligent but tender self-scrutiny. Healing trauma ain't for sissies. It requires stam-ina and the fortitude to stare into the eyes of the worst of the worst and not blink first.

Creepy old men are a cliché because they are everywhere. In parks, in stores, in families, up the street. I know I'm not the only one who can't hear the leering chorus of "Thank Heaven for Little Girls" with-out getting a major pedophilic quease. Not that little boys are spared. There are plenty of creeps to go around for anybody with purity just waiting to be snatched.

I had long suspected that wandering hands and bad boundaries were part of my early childhood. Once I was in the safe cradle of matrimony, things went completely to the dumps and the truth about my childhood slithered out. I hadn't even been married for two years when my father passed away after a debilitating illness, and whatever sense of protection I'd gleaned from him evaporated in a blink. I grew hostile, emotionally itchy, and claustrophobic as post-traumatic stress came boiling out. I left my husband rather abruptly, running like an escaped animal, and we lived apart for sixteen months while I got to the bottom of what made me flee our home as if being chased. When I, in the sunlit bedroom of my sublet apartment, finally connected the feelings to the facts, recalling a scene where the old-man babysitter made a grab at me, then shook me like a cloth doll and threatened to kill me if I told, I sank into my laundry pile, like a Victorian maid on to a fainting couch. I had remembered—and truly felt—the horror, and from there, I began to rebuild. Years later, unexpected and unpro- voked, I saw, flat and bloodless as a movie still, the moment when he tried to inch beyond his violent fascination with me to a full-fare roaming fingers tour, although I was predisposed to brushing off the brunt of the violation with "Well, at least he stayed on the outside of my underwear."

So I knew a little bit about the patchy way that traumatic memories show themselves—a glimmer of thought here, a fleeting sensation or image there. Now the little signal blips that kept coming up as my deep, suicidal funk cleared spelled out in psychic Morse code, *Mom, Mom, Mom.* I desperately didn't want this depression to be about my mother. It would have been so much easier to direct all the blame to the creepy old guy who lived up the street. But I intuited a maternal mess burrowing under the feeling of not-rightness in my family, and that my latest spin into depression was like the ocular halo that comes on right before a migraine—a warning of pain yet to come.

Surfacing from under the foggy veil of depression was the dawn- ing realization that my mother might be mentally ill. Not just now, but all along—and that what seemed then like little idiosyncrasies were in fact a big, big deal. Funny how long it takes to see what's right in front of you.

When my father died in 2004, Mom moved into a retirement community, a bright, modern, two-bedroom rental apartment that became overtaken by clothes with tags still on from Mervyn's, Marshall's, and the Talbot's outlet, sink-rinsed underwear draped to dry over the bars of unused walkers, and cigarette butts stubbed out in empty tuna cans on the cluttered kitchen counter.

After recovering from lung cancer, my mother continued to smoke, despite her doctors and all of us kids begging her to do whatever it took to quit—nicotine patches, acupuncture and herbs, therapy, in-patient treatment. Her house, never tidy, became downright dangerous in its slovenliness. The spare bedroom, which she'd set up as an office, was stuffed so full of old newspapers, magazines, furniture, and junk that if she tripped on something, she could very easily fall and break her increasingly fragile back. The refrigerator held an epidemiologist's trove of mold growing on hardening cheese, on lunch meat, on unidentifiable hunks of leftovers in foil-topped plastic bowls. We suggested hiring a cleaning service or calling a professional organizer. Both were refused.

Just the thought of telling an ugly truth feels as if you might die, because honesty runs counter to the fictional narrative propping up the house. Instead of facing the truth about my family, I created excuses: Mom wasn't neglectful, she was just busy. The times when one of us kids had to be rushed to the hospital because Mom had hoped our asthma would resolve itself over the steam from a teakettle—who *wouldn't* wait it out? The filth? Well, five kids make for a messy house. The disagreements Mom and Dad had over her mess-making—or Dad going nuclear at the dinner table for no real reason beyond someone's spilled milk—well, all parents fight sometimes.

The empress and her emperor had no clothes, but everyone was too busy admiring the queenly cheekbones, the jewel-like sparkle of wit, the scepter of Ivy League favor, and all the other accessories of an allegedly happy family.

The traumatic affront was easier for me to name when the injury came from a stranger, not family; when the violation took place upon my body, not my mind; when the gory details were titillating and obviously perverse rather than plain old warped and perplexing and sad. Lack of malicious intent doesn't mean that no harm was done. Neglect is like the grey rape of trauma—it's hard to convince the skeptics, including yourself, that it was as bad as it was. Which is nonsense. There's no sign anywhere saying, "Your abuse must be *this* obvious to ride the roller coaster at Trauma Park."

I tell myself I'm afraid of people not believing anything traumatic happened to me, but in truth, *I* don't want to believe anything traumatic happened to me. I want to be tougher than trauma, to be emotionally fleet of foot enough to outrun any lasting damage, but I'm not.

My mom was a black-belt underminer. She was fiercely on my side, until she wasn't. We didn't have social position or a lot of money, but she did have the stereotypical WASP gift for deadpan with the lacerating efficacy of a bone saw. When I told her that my husband, Mike, and I were planning a formal post-deployment wedding, she said, her voice dry as a Cheever martini, "Oh? Are you planning to wear white?" This was among the softer slights she delivered, but it was the one when I finally realized it wasn't safe to talk to her without first girding my loins.

I never stopped wishing that I could rely on my mother and talk to her the way daughters are supposed to be able to—with a heart fully bared—but I couldn't. She could be counted on in an emergency, eventually, but if there was no storm in sight, she could be unbearably snide. When I visited or called home, I never knew which version of my mom was going to greet me. There are few things more confusing than loving someone whom you cannot trust.

The daughter of a teenage mother in Baltimore, back when that was a major scandal, my mom was raised by her grandparents, then shipped off to boarding school with her baby brother, Harvey, while their mother worked as an accountant. I never met my grandfather. My grandmother divorced him when my mother and uncle were toddlers, and alcoholism wiped him out young. My mother never talked about him. On the rare occasion we asked, she would shrink back; I could actually see her retreat behind her eyes, her irises the cool grey of steel security gates.

Coming of age handsome and slender in an era that valued pretty and curvy, my mother was not without her charm. Clever, bright, with a fearsome steel-trap mind for facts and quotes, she was, on her good days, fun and loving. I was always allowed to dig through her enormous cluttered handbags to look for stray butterscotch candies, and when she hugged me, she meant it. When she was happy, I could barely stand to be away from her. But she was often distracted, overwhelmed, and short-tempered, and over time, our home became more and more squalid. Unless you visited our house, you'd never know—my mother could be leaning against the kitchen sink for half an hour, cigarette burning down between her fingers, then, if the phone rang, she'd greet whomever was calling with a high, trilling voice that sounded sweet and wholesome as Doris Day perched on a swing in a magnolia tree.

Like many families in orbit around the unspeakable—alcoholism, drug abuse, scandal, violence, mental illness—ours was a tippy-toe clan. We wended through the emotional minefields the way we'd maneuver past the patches of dog pee on the brown shag living room rug in our Michigan house, covered in paper towels weighted down by big cans of tomato juice or knockoff Hi-C citrus punch or whatever. You never knew where the danger spots were until you stepped in one. Shouldn't parents housebreak a dog? Somehow, they never got around to dealing with it, so the seven of us learned to navigate around puddles of urine in the house. Avoidance was a team sport.

Everyone in a messed-up household has their assigned role. *Welcome to the family. Please read this script.* The roles we're assigned vary: Bad news. Superstar. Sensitive snowflake. Salt of the earth. Dutiful son. Naughty girl. But all child actors have something in common. We think we will be punished for two things: breaking character and telling the truth. We stay in line because a damaged family seems less frightening than no family at all. At least we know where we belong.

Rather than pointing out the family madness, we act it out: I was a noisy, temperamental, unkempt kid. Smart and theatrical, but resistant to any kind of structure. When I discovered punk rock, I found an art form and a philosophy I could attach to my own chaos and disarray. It sounded the way I felt. Of course, any history of acting out, coupled with depression, makes kids highly susceptible to any suggestion that we're crazy—a classic self-gaslighting maneuver. But we aren't crazy; we're honest. Nowadays a psychologist would call us the *identified patients*—the weirdos in the family who outwardly telegraph the dysfunction. Back then they just called us trouble.

In tippy-toe households, denial can be passed down through

generations. Evasions and lies are the family tradition. When we talked about ancestry—my grandparents and their parents—my parents never talked about the suicides, the drinkers, the verbal abuse and knocking around. But the shadows of them were there, and they had an incalculable effect. A voice whispered from within my depression, "Psst, honey? It's time to know what you know."

Trauma doesn't always look like a bombed-out village or a gun to the temple or a burglar in a mask. Sometimes it just looks like good old Mom and Dad. Add to this the natural protectiveness we feel toward family and loved ones—no matter how screwy—and one needs a long time to even name it. When there's genuine love and care and good memories layered in with the suck, it's hard to sort out. You rummage through the box, flipping over what you think are flower cards—family trips to the beach, reunions, holidays—and find fly-traps and stinging nettles and strangling vines instead.

For me, talking about trauma brings it back to life, as if by speaking it aloud, the shame and disgust will rise up and get me—speak of the devil and he appears—so I keep it out of conversation.

Or maybe the balancing act of coming forward as a victim of sexual abuse and parental neglect is too hard to reconcile. I don't want to be defined by it, but I never want the horror of it belittled either. I want the respect that my pain warrants, and yet, let's face it: *victim* is the qualifier nobody wants.

I longed to believe that some part of me went untouched, that whatever innocence I held hadn't been crumpled like a paper accordion. That I wasn't damaged and stained since the beginning—Lady Macbeth in Garanimals. But what stories do we tell ourselves around the pain that, scientific research tells us, settles into our very cells?

We're not worthy. We're not safe. We could've done better; we could've prevented it. We deserved it. We're not whole underneath it all.

Damage, damage, all the way down. Ruined for good.

Trauma survivors have lived, often for years, by our wits, relying on them for survival, so we're afraid to change the channel from the Emergency Broadcast System to tune into something higher, something *not us*. When nobody was there for you before, back when you were wedged in the hellmouth, it's hard to believe that God would be there for you now. Fall into the arms of mercy? Yeah, right.

Maybe you've been burned so badly by church, so you can't believe in "God." Can you believe in an Infinite Creator? Animating Presence? The Universe? Force for Good? Divine Spirit? The Great Wahoo? Maybe call it loving-kindness or greater peace or the flow.

Pastor Tim Keller said, in a sermon on how to endure hardship, "With Jesus, you have a God who suffers not only for you, but with you."[1] Hard as it was for me to believe these words, I held on to them like a tiny Linus blanket scrap. This notion of belonging among the broken beckoned me forward to put a little faith in faith, some trust in trust.

Even as I clung to the comfort of a suffering Jesus, I dreaded what he taught about the *F*-word: *forgiveness*. Someone once called trauma a "moral crime." How do you forgive people who have, through word or action—or neglect—altered your perception of the ethical landscape? Who have whittled away your innocence? I would no sooner tell someone to forgive an abuser than I would tell a child to kiss a

Bad Touch Uncle because it'd make him happy. And yet, there's Jesus saying, "Get a move on."

Every violated soul craves justice. Every wounded child deserves a fair accounting. No help toward those ends comes from the pious tin drum beating: *forgive forgive forgive.*

Some people—some deeply, impressively devout people, bless their hearts—will goad others into forgiving early and often. Thou shalt forgive, and thou shalt do it on my timeline, at my insistence. That's not what Jesus preaches; that's spiritual abuse cloaked in verse.

True forgiveness is organic, and its moment comes once the pain has completed its work. Sometimes attachment to resentment and inability to forgive is not stubbornness, but a sign that a more thorough accounting is needed. It is the victim's prerogative to withhold forgiveness until the scars have finished saying everything they need to say. Forgiveness that is rushed or forced isn't authentic forgiveness; it's performance art.

Once it arrives, forgiveness doesn't require reconciliation. The abuser doesn't necessarily get drawn back into the fold, or even invited out for coffee. Forgiveness means no longer waiting for the apology that will never come, the justice never served. Forgiveness means not letting the thought of what happened ruin your day. It means giving yourself the gift of peaceful hours whether those who hurt you cross your path, or cross your mind, or not. And if you find that you, personally, can't let the person who hurt you off the hook, you can leave it up to the guy on the cross. We pray for Jesus to forgive because it seems beyond our mortal reach; we pray for him to forgive because we can't sue our parents for malpractice.

There can be a beautiful circularity in forgiving a neglectful or angry parent—or so I hoped. They gave you life; you give them clemency. But I don't know about forgiving those who sexually prey upon others. The recidivism rate is awfully high. I rarely think about my friendly neighborhood groper, and I'm sure he's deceased by now, so I guess that bit of business is done. But regarding those who must heal from violators still among us, I do know this: you can forgive *and* keep your distance. In fact, I advise it.

I don't want to be a resident of Trauma Town, but now when a fellow citizen shows up, raw and skittish and battle-scarred, I can pay forward the sacred gift of "Me too." I can't change what happened; I can only change how I carry it now.

Trauma begs for a witness and a trustworthy hand to hold when it is shaken from its box of safekeeping, waiting to be matched. It's hard work to even contemplate. I once asked My Sister the Minister why life was so hard, and she said, "Because we're not meant to do it alone." That's where Jesus comes in—as someone to lean on with my shame and secrets. As someone to keep me company while I sort it all out. Psalm 119:50 says, "This is my comfort in my affliction, that your promise gives me life."

In *War and Peace,* Tolstoy wrote that "the two most powerful warriors are patience and time."[2] So we can know we are warriors, even when we're moving only one tiny step at a time toward healing, on hesitant cat paws. And we need not do it alone. If you can, picture this: Sitting next to you on the edge of the pit, feet dangling, Jesus weeps. A loving witness. A force for mercy to whom you can say, "The worst of the worst has happened." He will turn his scarred wrists outward and say, "Me too."

Patience with others is difficult. Patience with yourself is harder still. But if you keep turning the cards over, you see that the pieces that seemed so ill-assorted are actually perfectly mated: terror with holy presence; patience with time; assigned accountability and, perhaps, forgiveness. Enjoy this mix-and-match, paradoxical beauty; it is yours to keep, the prize for the labor of your nerve. The pieces are coming together now, forming a radiant whole.

6

⋇

JOYFUL NOISE

Again with the crying. I was in the car alone, fingers sweeping my tear-starred eyelashes like wiper blades so I could see the sunny road in front of me. Through the film of my tears, the pavement seemed to sparkle. I shouldn't have been crying on such a beautiful day.

Driving and crying seemed to have become my secret, second life. Sometimes I cried because I was moved by the music and sometimes I cried because the lyrics touched me, but mostly I cried because underneath the eggshell veneer of capability and purpose, I was scared, confused, and generally discombobulated, and a good cry is how I become emotionally organized. Music is the spine that straightens it all out.

Before I had God, I had music. Or maybe they're the same thing. I tend to think they are.

In grade school, I was an okay student when I felt good, but my strongest subject was truancy. Starting in first grade, I looked for excuses to sit at home and tune in to the radio, alternating between daydreaming and thinking about how messed up the world was and what I might do to change it.

When I'm depressed, my capacity for pleasure takes a hike. The world goes grey—joyless and flavorless, one big bowl of wheat-paste gruel. I become Sisyphus with a case of the Mondays. I revert to my kid-self: sad, frustrated to the point of trip-wire rage, and wanting nothing but the solitude of sitting cross-legged on my bed, rocking back and forth, listening to eardrum-battering music through headphones. Only now that I'm older—somewhere between "Gabba Gabba Hey!" and "Get off my lawn!"—my ears ring and my knees start to ache.

When we need healing hands, songs are nurses. When we feel alone, songs are friends.

When I was a kid, and sometimes even as an adult, I'd poke myself with safety pins or draw something sharp along my skin to see if I could still feel. Going so far to evoke sensation seems unnecessarily extreme to me now—I didn't have to cut myself. I could have put on a song I love, and that same tidal flood of feeling would've gushed right forth, rich as blood.

By high school I had my own bedroom. I also had the Sex Pistols, the Dead Kennedys, and The Cure on vinyl, as well as an anarchist politic around which to wrap my rage. My dad had become less the angry Willy Loman figure of my early youth, and more a post-Depression childhood survivor made glad by leisurely afternoons cruising grocery outlets to buy cut-price glazed donuts and picking through junkyards to find parts for his disintegrating blue Ford Falcon. He finally got rid of the old beast when you could count the highway stripes through the holes rusted in the driver-side floorboard.

My mom was starting to slip further away. After I rocketed out of my New Jersey bedroom through my headphones, listening to songs of smashing the state and romancing the dark, I'd wake up for school each weekday morning at 6:15, fifteen minutes before the school bus chugged into our development, afraid I'd find her drowned in the tub after having fallen asleep, again, during her bath. I'd crack the hollow-core door to the bathroom, which would make her eyes snap open. She'd sit up slowly, her wet hair sluicing back, reminding me, horribly, of the zombie woman in the bathroom scene from *The Shining*. But at least she woke up. Whew.

I saved all my money from babysitting and housecleaning and clerking in a goldenrod-and-brown smock at ShopRite to buy records and concert tickets. I watched David Bowie perform "Space Oddity" in a huge arena, feeling as though my alien kin were reaching right between my ribs in recognition, my body a tiny dot as far from the stage as Major Tom floated above the Earth. I saw the Ramones in a moshing Jersey roil that had the jet-speed, affirming love-force of a three-chord family reunion. Later, when I moved to New York City, I went to a special midnight Prince show where his extended encore of "Purple Rain" was so trippy and ascendant that we all but left our bodies. That tiny guy in the high-heeled boots was a holy man; anyone in the audience that night would swear it.

Punk and Goth allegiance aside, musically, I've always enjoyed my guilty pleasures. I love easy-listening ballads with their button-busting declarations of devotion and heartbreak layered over strings and sad piano, and metal anthems with shredding guitar that swear to bend the world to their will. Middlebrow music is my favorite when I'm down, and I have a scale of genres that tracks how bad I'm feeling: there's ABBA Bad, Patsy Cline Bad, Carpenters Bad, and at the very bottom, when I'm as low as I can go and want to curl up in a ball with a package of Oreos, is the stage known as Manilow Bad. The first album I ever bought with my own money was by Barry Manilow, and he has crooned the crease out of my worried brow with "I Made It Through the Rain" more times than I can count.

But a new obsession brings a blush to my cheek to confess. You can snoop through my computer's browser history or do some recon on the secret snack stash in my highest kitchen cabinet, but I'd be mortified if you checked out my iTunes playlist, for it is full of Christian Contemporary—an overwhelmingly white, overproduced genre of radio-friendly praise music.

A basic taxonomy of Christian Contemporary lyrics has three categories: "I'm in a Monogamous Relationship with God," "Four Minutes About How Jesus Saves," and, my favorite, "Help Me, Lord, for I Am So, So Screwed." Driving around crying to "I'm So Screwed" songs reminded me of what I sought in God, not to be made new, but perhaps made 17 percent less awful.

Depression is, at its core, a deficit of hope. These songs—aching in their sincerity—offered company for my misery, and hope for repair that I could hear, if not yet hold on to. Casting Crowns, MercyMe, Chris Tomlin, Newsboys, Jeremy Camp, Third Day—so many artists that sang my heart back to me. Listen to Danny Gokey singing "Give Me Jesus" backed by a gospel choir, and tell me you don't feel just a little bit redeemed.

"A song will outlive all sermons in the memory," said Henry Giles,[1] and I can wring more hope and meaning out of a four-minute song than out of all the church I've attended in my lifetime. Where words fail, music makes a way. I'll get in the car, on the verge of zipping back into my hard-hided alligator suit, then the right Christian contemporary song will come on, and—in four bars or less—I'm a stuffed bunny in the basket of God's love.

I drove and drove and drove, Palisades Parkway and I-84 and Orrs Mills Road, doing blacktop therapy—these songs my road back to a clean spiritual slate and an innocence that passed me by. The Welsh have a word for it—*hiraeth*—meaning, roughly, homesickness for a home that never was. If I had any hope at all of rising above the black tide, I'd have to let the waves break over me. These singers had been there, and they made it hurt a little less.

I broadened my playlist of inspirationals, now as moved by Stevie Wonder's "Higher Ground" as old spirituals like "Many Rivers to Cross" and Indigo Girls' gritty "Closer to Fine." And, like everybody else, I love Leonard Cohen's "Hallelujah"—perhaps the modern age's finest secular hymn (often heard when worshipping at Our Lady of Starbucks). The broken hallelujah chorus of that song heals us all, a collective revival. Let's not be stingy in our interpretation here. If your spirit is awakened by "Eye of the Tiger," who am I to judge? Any song is a hymn if you love it enough.

I punctuated each wobbly step back toward faith with song. Then I punctuated each wobbly step with punctuation. A semicolon, to be precise. A young Christian named Amy Bleuel came forward with Project Semicolon and changed how I saw myself. Amy battled addiction, mental illness, self-harm, and suicidal thoughts after her father died by his own hand when she was only eighteen years old.

Bleuel honored her dad's memory by getting a small tattoo of a semicolon. Then she developed Project Semicolon, a faith-based non-profit that encourages and supports people who suffer from depression, addiction, self-harm, and thoughts of self-injury or suicide.

The group explains the significance of this particular punctuation: "A semicolon is used when an author could've chosen to end their sentence, but chose not to. The author is you and the sentence is your life."[2] Started in 2013, Project Semicolon garnered worldwide attention, and the semicolon tattoo concept went viral as a symbol of solidarity.

"When the foundation of this project was created those involved reflected on what got them to where they are today. The answer was clear that it was the love of Christ," Bleuel wrote on the Project Semicolon website. "As we set forth in the project, we committed to loving with a Christ-like love those who are struggling. We inspire others through the very thing that brought us to continuance in our own stories. This by no means excludes any other beliefs or religions, as we accept them all."[3]

Punctuation as resurrection. I loved it.

Some depressives can go full crank even when they feel like garbage: "I was so terrifically depressed while I was getting my second PhD after medical school at Stanford . . ." Not me; I'm a dead-stop depressive. When my illness is really bad, I am toast by the time I finish making my bed. *If* I can make my bed that day.

Medication helped. My SSRI prescription gave me enough juice to get up and get dressed. But music filled in where medicine left off—shifting that dreaded feeling of deficiency and aloneness. And the semicolon metaphor reminded me, as Reverend Kim had said, that pain isn't the end of the story.

On bad days, I'd drive around itemizing why I sucked: *I didn't finish high school, and forget about college. I'm selfish. I'm a horrible, worthless person.* Then a favorite oldie would come on—*Ooooob, "Dancing Queen"!*—and my mood would lift. Music gave me a needed boost, like an old friend dropping by unexpectedly, and I could make it through another day. Sometimes songs aren't just medicine. Sometimes songs are semicolons too.

But in a semicolon season, how do you find interest in living?

The answer is "very, very slowly." Being restored by grace isn't some flash-bang magic show miracle, like the wave of a wand and a poof of glittery smoke that makes the pretty girl sawn in two become whole again. It's more like renovating an old house: Peeling off old siding, piece by piece. Replacing rotten planks in the floor. Plugging holes with wood patch. Putting on a ventilator and scraping away the old lead paint of toxic emotional patterns. My own restoration moved along at a snail's pace, and it took thoroughness and patience that rivaled any mother's love. I had to parent myself back to habitability. When it all seemed to be going too slowly, or poorly, I put the music on, crawling into the sanctuary of song. In a life shuttered behind shame and confusion and regret, my embrace of music, my obsession with it, lets in some cleansing sunlight. The right song coming on the radio at the right time—as if God were the DJ—can make you feel downright blessed.

One afternoon on a praise drive, I pulled up to a stoplight and saw some glorious fool howling along to Journey's "Don't Stop Believing" while waiting for the light to change. I've also caught a beetle-browed bro yelling to Kanye, hogging the sidewalk as he swaggered by in white boy rap-along ecstasy. I see lots of women in SUVs popping their gum as their ponytails bounce to some kind of magic coming from the car speakers, the kids in the backseat, oblivious to Mom's euphoric jam. I never know what they're listening to, but I always assume they're healing. A fist pump along to a beat may be the first swing in a comeback fight for life.

Music connects us to source, and to each other. I adore how evangelical we can be about our favorite songs: You can express marginal interest in a band that someone likes, and they will deliver a mix tape or custom-made playlist for you within a day. *You have to check this out.* Communion.

Songs have sacred power, restoring us three, four, five blessed minutes at a time. A song says, "Keep going. You can do this. Crawl on your bloodied knees if you have to, and I'll sing you home. Don't stop believing." We can hit the replay button as many times as we need—rock out, shout along. We can weep until we're cleansed. We can let the music move us until our wounded hearts start healing and our broken hallelujah sounds like church.

7

※

SELF-IMPROVEMENT
FOR JERKS

You know what's annoying? When some doofus has to ruin something you enjoy by mentioning how they did it first. Like, *ages* ago.

So let me tell you how I started doing yoga way before it was cool.

When I began my yoga practice as a teenager in the East Village, yoga was for oddballs. Now it's the scoffed-at spiritual pursuit of Basics in stretchy pants—an army of shopping mall "Spiritual Gangsters" reaching into warrior pose in search of a higher plane and a perkier butt. I'm actually okay with this. Turns out, I'm pretty basic, too, and those pants are supremely comfortable.

Still, I did not want to be the white, artsy, bourgeois lady in yoga pants stretching and bending her way to inner peace. That is so not my vibe. Yet there I sat, cross-legged on a pale green mat, eyes closed in the local strip mall yoga studio, ignoring the teacher's dharma talk in favor of cringing at the ricochet of scolding, weasely thoughts pinging around my skull: *You should've done this sooner. The teacher asked you to quiet your mind, and here you are, brain clacking away like a set of those chattering windup teeth. What's wrong with you? You can't even do self-improvement right, you idiot.*

I hate trying to relax. It's so stressful.

Among the more reasonable objections to Christianity is aversion to a "prayer fixes everything" mentality, which, let me tell you, isn't a big hit with us churchy types who rely on medication for emotional stability. I consider taking my medicine an act of service. As Glennon Doyle Melton wrote, "Jesus loves me this I know, for he gave me Lexapro."[1]

Yes, Lord. Give us this day our daily meds.

Even with medication, there is still work to do on the old jalopy. The drugs gave me the feeling of having brake pads again, instead of metal screeching against metal when the pedal was mashed to the floor, but I had no lasting sense of inner resources. No spiritual survival plan. Luck, it turns out, is not a plan. Go figure. But bringing everything to a grinding halt wasn't an option; I'd have to fix this car while I was driving it.

So I started yoga again.

Just as you can't pray your way to mental health if your brain chemistry is out of whack, you can't beat a sense of struggling isolation and futility all alone. The worst thoughts and moods move on, yet depression leaves behind a grimy film of loathing. Trauma and depression actually reshape your brain, morphing your neural pathways from a system of passable, mostly peaceful roads into a snarl of switchbacks and hairpin turns in which all manner of emotional traffic gets piled up.

A lifetime of mental logjam turned me into a major awfulizer—the smallest setback could trigger a spiral effect that would send me downward into despair and defensiveness, which, over time, turned anxiety into a reflex. Worrying is my cardio.

My husband—my patient, analytical husband, who due to both his nature and his profession can be counted upon to consider all future outcomes—observed that my constant catastrophizing would eventually become a self-fulfilling prophecy. We see what we look for. He somehow managed to survive making that point, which, given my hair-trigger defenses, was not guaranteed. He held his hands up—"Don't shoot!" style—as he said it, prefaced by "This isn't a criticism!" Depression is not the most endearing affliction—I'm agitated as often as I'm blue. But I did, against my own doubting nature, listen to him.

The body—that flawed, magnificent container we each rattle around in—seems suspiciously absent as a focus in Christianity, except as a vehicle of sin. This makes me nervous, as if the only skin-to-skin contact worth exalting were the touch of a hand to the cover of a leather Bible. Yoga, by contrast, aims to bring all aspects of the self together—body, mind, and spirit—the word *yoga* meaning "union" in Sanskrit.

Among some Christians, practicing yoga is controversial. I Googled "Can Christians do yoga," and the search returned almost thirteen million hits. Thirteen million articles, debates, threads, and posts all kicking around whether or not yoga, with its roots in Hinduism, was cheating on Jesus. Wow. And my favorite class was on Sunday mornings too. I hadn't foreseen this conflict. I decided, guiltily, to take my chances and swap time in the pew for time on the mat when I felt the need.

Forget doing a split, or tucking your ankles behind your neck, or standing on your head. The most difficult part of yoga is getting to yoga. Once I got to class, kicked off my shoes, unrolled my sticky mat on the wood floor of the classroom, and sat down, things became easier. All I had to do was pay attention, listen, move according to the gentle guidance, and trust.

I had to practice focusing on the teacher's dharma talk instead of my thoughts, which remained a confusing racket, noisy as the chatter in an air-traffic controller's headphones. All those voices on all those different frequencies, squawking at once: worry, anxiety, tasks, to-dos, regrets, physical aches and pain, endless internal commentary about my weight and my shape.

Then I started to get obnoxious, mocking myself as I leaned into a triangle pose or an awkward chair. I'd imagine a voice-over, like Carrie Bradshaw on *Sex and the City*, while I bent this way and that: "As I did yoga in this room full of middle-class white people, I couldn't help but wonder: Did God have a glorious plan for my life?"

Sarcasm is my sign that I'm anxious, angry, or tired. It's basically self-righteousness with a laugh track. At one point, Frannie, my biker buddy, called me on it. "You ever heard of a condition called *terminal uniqueness*? It's when you think you're *so* special and *so* smart and your troubles are *so* much different from everyone else's . . ."

"So, so, so . . . so, what?" I said, incriminated into monosyllables.

"I'm just saying that stuff is deadly."

"How?"

"I've seen it over and over again. People who think they're above it all . . . they've seen it all before, heard it all before, and there's nothing anybody else can teach them, so they build a big defensive wall between themselves and everyone else, and they end up worse than when they started. Some of 'em end up dead."

"What's your point?"

"I'm trying to tell you that there's such a thing as being, actually, too cool to live."

As if to show me that God, too, had a sense of humor and that it was okay to get off my hipper-than-thou high horse and get with the program, Leslie, one of my favorite teachers, shared with me that she moonlights from her regular job as a Presbyterian minister. Slender, redheaded, with a face that crinkled into the cutest of smiles as she taught, Leslie was big into the mind-body connection, always encouraging students to consider how our emotions affect our physical states: our issues in the tissues.

Rather than bully the body into submission, Leslie suggested letting the body lead the way. "It is far easier to act your way to right thinking," she said, "than to think your way to right acting." I had to hear this about a dozen times before I could figure out what it meant—that you can't always think or will your way to a solution or an inner shift. You act your way toward it, by doing what you think is the next right thing, or the thing right in front of you, or by letting your gut guide you with the feeling that lies just beyond your fear.

Still, I'd attack myself in yoga class. *You suck* as a mantra is rather unproductive; not to mention, it runs counter to point. But I didn't have anything better in mind except to tell myself to relax, which turned out to be as helpful as someone saying "Calm down!" when you're angry. To people with control issues like mine, relaxing seems appealing but also scary.

My friend Jen is terrified of flying, and once when I met her at the airport, she came to meet me by the luggage carousel all flipped out. Her husband said, "Excuse her. She's exhausted from keeping the plane in the air." Why we view worry as productive, I don't know. Maybe we figure that by digging our nails into our palms (or into a plane seat's armrest) we know what to do with our hands.

I was also concerned that yoga might turn me into some overly chill bohemian boob who chanted while Rome burned. If you're used to fighting for survival, the thought of mellowing out seems not only impossible but devastating. If the fight were taken out of me, who would I be?

I once watched a news segment about a California spa clinic that offered high colonics—a sort of Roto-Rooter wherein your insides are irrigated by a stream of water pumped into your lower GI tract. One client—a very spaced-out, well-groomed middle-aged woman— talked about getting a colonic every week in conjunction with her strict juice fasts. "Every time I come here, I'm getting closer to spirit. To who I really am," she said. I remember thinking that I don't know if I'll find God, but I'd prefer not to extend the search up my own behind.

For its challenges, Christianity never seemed flaky. But did my return to Christianity knock out any other spiritual practices as con- tenders? Leslie made me feel better about two-timing Jesus, though my Sundays were split: Should I go to church or go to yoga class? Did dividing my Sundays mean I was dividing my loyalty?

I started going to Leslie's Monday morning class instead. There I noticed a familiar-looking bearded guy on the mat behind me, wriggling his way into high lunge, his arms reaching overhead. It was

Ben, the pastor of Beacon's First Presbyterian Church. Seeing him in class absolved me of any conflict. It was okay to be a student of the gospel with a minor in yoga.

My first yoga studio was in a basement on Avenue B, the air heavily perfumed with Nag Champa incense burning in the curve of a silver-bellied abalone shell on the altar. The other students were punks and burnouts and artists and leftover hippie seekers who'd moved into the neighborhood when it was a no-man's-land of tumbledown abandoned buildings, drugs, and guns. I'd drop into that basement and perfect my backbend until my platinum hair extensions trailed on the floor beneath me. My headstands felt funny when I shaved my hair into a Mohawk, as if I had a carpet strip running down the center of my skull as I balanced, my legs slicing through the air. I was flexible and angry, troubled but low on worldly cares.

Yoga gave me the first glimpses of the terror that resided in the hollow of my heart. Whenever I'd arch back over my bent elbows in fish pose, expanding my rib cage so fully my heart felt exposed, I'd have horrible flashback-like visions of being knifed between my ribs. The vulnerability of openness terrified me. The head may think it keeps the most accurate record of things, but it's the body that knows. The body knows.

Still, I loved my teachers (I never did call them *gurus*) and they loved me, offering me encouragement, affection, and even a job managing the neighborhood café that one of them owned. I saw myself as a dropout scrub, but in their eyes, a gloomster like me could be a source of light, and I was grateful. They becalmed and emboldened me. In a way, that yoga crew was my first real faith community. A portrait of Jesus was propped on the altar next to the Indian gurus who'd guided them, and these teachers made me feel seen and loved. Chosen.

But I wasn't that punk kid any longer. I was just another lady of a certain age trying to do a forward bend without groaning. I wasn't special. I wasn't badass. I was simply a woman who had lost years to an affliction that I had assumed for too long was just the way I was. Years I will never get back. I know everyone has their pain, and there's no hierarchy of suffering, but I'd resent my depression so much less if it hadn't cost me so much damn time.

Still, for all her sneering nihilism, that punk rock girl still lived inside me. If I could call on her furious hope, she'd help me fight toward a future.

You cannot, however, fight toward a future until you learn how to effectively inhabit the here and now. This odious detail is wedged into the fine print.

When I do yoga, I tend to fixate on the students in class who make it look effortless, seeming to master poses in mere seconds, while I'm wobbling to maintain balance and spitting away the strands of hair that have fallen loose from my ponytail and gotten stuck in my lip balm. A good yoga teacher will instruct you to keep your focus on your own mat, to not be overly preoccupied with the people breathing and sweating right next to you. As instructed, I watch my thoughts: *Oh, that girl was skinny already anyway. And limber. That guy was probably a gymnast as a kid. Man, I suck at this. I want his flexibility, her hundred-dollar yoga pants, her Tree of Life tattoo, and her peppy glutes.* Until I finally take hold of my jumping monkey mind and bring the focus back to me and my mat. There are better ways to spend precious minutes than to bitterly compare my interior mess to someone's exterior polish.

The Bible tells you the story of God's purpose for humanity, but yoga helps you edit and rewrite the story you tell yourself. The practice moves you into a better headspace: an elegant and efficient process of rewiring. A place of calm between your ears. The head as an oasis, not a snakepit. What a concept.

Psalm 46:10 says, "Be still, and know that I am God," but I couldn't tell which was more difficult: the being still or the knowing.

On a glass shelf in the corner of the yoga studio sits a tiny plant, a philodendron, its green tendrils curling along the sides of its glass vase, roots dangling and floating free in the water. There is nothing in which to ground itself, yet the plant grows anyway.

Yoga teacher Liz, a cerebral and unreasonably foxy mother of three, said in a dharma talk that "what you resist persists." I tucked this away, an aphoristic stone in my pocket that I'd rub as a reminder. There's a strain of theological snobbery that denigrates slogans, but they have their utility, which happens to be the same reason they are criticized—because they are simple. Sometimes a slogan is all the battered brain can handle. A purist priest may scoff at slogans because he or she is dogmatically positioned against "all the truth that can fit on a bumper sticker." But when we're really in the muck, we can barely retain all the truth that can fit on a Post-it note.

The more I resisted anxiety and depression and self-loathing, the more it would pop up, bogeyman–style, to show itself. I had to accept that I was going to be down in the mud, alligator-wrestling my brain a bit longer than I'd like. I wouldn't necessarily get back up when I wanted; I'd get back up when it was time.

After class, Liz motioned me aside. On her ankle, she had a tattoo of the blue triangular symbol for the fifth chakra—the energy center of clear communication and self-expression. "Listen," she said, "the mother in me wants to ask you to spit out your gum during class." I blushed. Sometimes I'd be so tense that I had to pop two sticks of Extra before I got on the mat. Liz understood and suggested that as a restless, headstrong type, I might find meditation helpful. I'd tried it before during my separation from Mike, but I gave it up in frustration when I couldn't stop my mind from skating back toward negative thoughts. The mind was simply too forceful a creature to quiet. I knew, though, that coming up with other things to do was more a means of distraction than anything else. Theologian Dr. Thema Bryant-Davis calls out diversion-as-evasion like this: "We run from inner stillness because we are afraid to remember the things we stay busy to forget. Busy does not equal healed."[2]

Why not give it another shot?

At home, I put on some quiet, exotic music, sat still, rested my hands palms-down on my knees, and closed my eyes.

What a disaster.

The advice for meditation novices is, if you find yourself thinking or your mind wandering, guide it back to nothingness. Easier said than done. I'd chase a thought like a dog after a speeding car, then bark at myself, *Thinking!* which set off a brush fire of self-hatred and loathing, every regret marching forth as if on cue.

I got the suggestion to ditch a formal mantra in favor of "Let go. Let go, let go, let go." "Let" on the inhale, "go" on the exhale. It was as if "Let go and let God" had subtly shifted shape to see if it might slip past my defenses. If the thoughts came parading by, instead of yelling at myself, I'd think, *Oh, hey, you're thinking,* then watch the thought float away like mist. It sounded so corny I couldn't stand it, but it worked. Gentleness: a swifter and more effective solution than brute force. Who knew?

I tossed the brain weasels a visual treat of a pink lotus floating on a still pond to keep them from running amok in a state of deprivation. Then I visualized a glowing crescent moon reflected over the ripples of an ink-dark sea, and I watched it fade like a watercolor wash as I brought my mind back to a blank canvas.

I lasted three minutes.

They were three very useful, calming, revitalizing minutes, I had to admit. I had more energy for the next couple of days, more clarity, and I even slept better. My brain weasels quieted down. When you're used to hard-charging and overextending and shoving things through the pipeline, carving out quiet time to tend to mind and body seems quite silly, possibly even counterproductive. The province of the soft and the self-obsessed. But feeling the positive effects of meditation and yoga forced me to examine my addiction to hustle. Said meditating hip-hop mogul Russell Simmons: "I used to think anxiety and insomnia drove me to success. But it was the stillness that let me be good at anything."[3]

On Sundays when I took class, I'd drive down the winding rural highway ten miles from the yoga studio to a Franciscan community built into a hillside. Just off the road where it curves round a wooded bend sits a quiet Shrine to Our Lady of Atonement. In the entry stands a large statue of Madonna and Child on a pedestal, Mary's gaze downcast and radiating supreme tenderness. The statue has always transfixed me, as if it holds some divine maternal magnetism.

Rarely would I see another person at the shrine, though occasionally I'd run into a puttering nun. I started dropping by weekly to check in, in a "call your mom" kind of way. Figures: the kid with the suboptimal mother wanted the best mother, the heavenly mother—Occam's Holy Razor. Mary, revered worldwide, even in non-Christian cultures, is the maternal figure who never harms or withholds or abandons or gets lost in her own madness. There are no broken promises here. No rejection. No pain. Just limitless love and compassion. A place of solace and peace beyond all understanding.

I stepped into the dark stone chamber and took a look around. There is nothing so sincere as a shrine—no ironic remove, kitsch, or pulled punches. In the room, bare but for statues of saints and black wrought-iron votive stands filled with simple tall white candles in glass, the spectrum of human emotion was palpable: Pain. Hope. Love. Need. Joy. Sorrow. The big stuff laid bare under Mary's gentle gaze. At her feet was arrayed a faded rainbow of flowers—sprays of gladiola, bouquets of gerbera daisies, single carnations in stem vases, and so many roses.

Roses, the privileged symbol of the Heavenly Mother, are said to miraculously bloom in the presence of a saint, and here they were abundant, in vases and on sills. Pink, white, yellow, red—which blooms were genuine and which were fake? Did it matter? The faith behind their offering was real.

I pushed a folded five-dollar bill into the slot in the lid of the care-worn white metal donation box and picked a long, slender wooden matchstick from the selection. The dark, dense air was warmed by the lit candles, every prayer manifested in the shimmering flames and held in their heat. I chose the candle on the top right of the rack near the prayer bench and knelt.

I felt foolish and exposed, the wood bench hard against my knees there in the dim candle-glow. But no voice called out, "Imposter!" No hand grasped my shoulder to pick me up and spin me out of the cavelike darkness and into the accusing morning light.

I prayed for the people hurting in my life, and I prayed for my sanity. *Please, God, my sanity.* Then at the very end, I bowed my forehead to my clasped praying hands and whispered aloud the most extreme words I could imagine. "Your will, not mine." For the first time, out loud, this control freak had turned everything over. *Thy will be done. Amen.*

I stood, dusted off my knees, and turned from the room. A candle might not fix everything, but it was a start in turning back the dark. On the way past the statue of Mary, I kissed my fingers and touched her bare plaster foot where it emerged from under her sky blue robe. *Here goes nothing.*

I felt grounded yet weightless, and for the first time in a long time, utterly sane. Relieved of a certain weight. I realized then that the point of enlightenment was not to become smarter, but, examining the word itself, to become lighter.

As a gesture, lighting a candle feels hopelessly small and huge at once. A classic rookie move, and also one of last resort, but you don't light a candle if you don't somehow believe. "Can't hurt, might help" is its own degree of commitment—how a recovering agnostic buys in. We build altars to create spaces that are not only sacred but also safe, and we illuminate them so Spirit can find the way to us. Among our offerings are words written on bits of paper, the vow of our presence, and the bounty of our gardens.

There's a no-nonsense sublimity to a shrine—to take our troubles, our hopes, and our hearts and lay them, like a soldier's captive arms, at Mary's feet. Along with the serenity of a shrine is its stability: We are welcome dawn to dusk. We need only to accept that the invitation is always open. We can wander away and then back again with the most tentative steps, and leave our cares in a room full of roses.

8

THE NED FLANDERS EFFECT

If you want to discern my faith, don't look around my neck for a cross. Just look at my Facebook page and you'll see how much I adore a good Jesus meme.

One of my favorites features a classic painting of villagers staring heavenward. "Jesus is coming," says the caption. "Look busy." Another: Jesus doing a facepalm with the caption: "Guys, I said I hate *figs*."

These may seem like jokes from the darkest side of sacrilege, but they get a good laugh, a click of the like button, and approving prayer-hands emoji from progressive Christians like me.

In the current political climate, sharing a meme that substitutes *figs* for a homophobic slur may not seem like much, but it's a protest none-theless. As is posting the meme that says: "Just once, the world would like to see Christians claim 'religious liberty' compelling us to feed children or curb gun violence or combat cancer or anything remotely life-affirming. Instead we use it to withhold wedding cakes . . ." My online activism is a way of communicating that I refuse to fall for the con, that I know full well that "religious liberty" legislation is not the stuff of protecting faith, but of pointing fingers.

I move mostly in the world of "nones," otherwise known as the "spiritual-but-not-religious." Many of them don't look kindly on Christians; they don't even think they know any.

According to the Pew Research Center, *none* is "the single most common religious identity among those born between 1980 and 2000." In the United States, the study projects, Christians will decline from more than three-quarters of the population in 2010 to two-thirds in 2050, while *nones* will increase from 17.1 percent to 25.6 percent in the same time period.[1]

So I sometimes feel I'm on the wrong side of history, and that makes me self-conscious about opening conversations about faith. But sharing posts, memes, and tweets makes me feel as though I might be able to, at the very least, let the nones know that Christianity isn't what they may think it is. The schism in Christianity these days runs far deeper than arguing over the pros and cons of accepting offerings online, or whether or not playing Christian rock during services constitutes pandering to Millennials.

The schism is this: the Ku Klux Klan, it has been reported, wants you to start thinking of it as a Christian group.[2] And a recent *Washington Post*/ABC poll revealed that American Christians, more than the nonreligious, are likely to support torture.[3] Also, there's good old Parson Trump, bungling a Corinthians reference in one breath and condemning immigrants in the next. The old hippie folk hymn paraphrasing John 13:35 says: "They will know we are Christians by our love." Love? Not based on my news feed.

The Christian Right in America has dozens of politicians and megapastors broadcasting its beliefs. Meanwhile, moderate Christians hardly make the media radar. Into that void, we're left with posting memes and retweeting actor John Fugelsang: "If you're a Christian American who discriminates against others, you suck at being Christian. And American."[4]

Moderate and progressive Christian activism doesn't make headlines, and it's certainly not clickbait. The basic goodness in my corner of Christianity garners pretty much no mainstream media attention. Crazy gets more clicks, so the extremists get all the airplay. The progressive message needs a signal boost.

Once I started posting Jesus memes, I realized I wasn't facing anti-Christian bias on the part of my friends, but simple ignorance. They had formulated their ideas about modern Christianity from what the media was telling them. To them, *Christian* equaled climate-change denier and homophobe. Was I one of those people? they wondered. They needed assurances that I didn't see faith and science, or even faith and common sense, as mutually exclusive. It was up to me to inform them that I was down with Bill Nye, not Lou Sheldon.

Then things got interesting. They'd quiz me: Those Christian business owners who refused, on religious grounds, to make wedding cakes or pizzas for same-sex couples—what would Jesus do? My answer: he'd start baking. (Could we have foreseen the culture wars being waged on a battlefield of carbs?) So, yes, social media can be a useless time suck, but it can also be a conduit for understanding.

I am aware of how trivial a Gospel According to Likes may seem: too personalized, as if the message were tantamount to a spiritual selfie—lamentations from the Church of Me. I know that when I retweet @UnvirtousAbbey—"For places where it's easier to get a gun than to get a job, we pray"—I may be merely affirming that I am not alone in my sadness about how my religion is being continually, devastatingly distorted.

If we want something to change, we start where we are, and where I am so often is online. The Bible says, "Judge not, that you be not judged" (Matthew 7:1). It doesn't say, "Let Bible-justified cruelty, prejudice, or downright nuttiness go unchallenged."

If I were to select just one social media message to communicate the outrage and sorrow I feel about the co-opting of Christianity, which hashtag, meme, or emoji would I choose?

That's easy.

#JesusWept.[5]

And yet, one can't only proselytize online. At some point, I realized I was going to have to claim my Christianity in person.

I sat at the diner's melamine-topped table across from my friend Trina, a halo of blue and violet neon reflected behind her head in the glare of the mirrored wall. We'd ordered omelets from the spiral-bound laminated menus—spinach and feta for me, vegetarian with a side of fruit instead of potatoes for her.

What is it about the American diner that so closely resembles a confessional? I have told more difficult truths propped up in a vinyl-upholstered booth, with a plate of fries in front of me, than I have anyplace else. Breakups, dropouts, freak-outs—most of these milestones schemed or admitted in close proximity to a Pepsi sign and a rotating dessert case full of brightly lit pies and cakes, topped with chocolate curls, shaved coconut, or Maraschino cherries. Maybe the emotional gates are opened because of the grounding, elemental pleasure of comfort food; maybe the shiny chrome trim and friendly service make you feel safe enough to speak your heart. I know that a little down-home touch makes me feel cared for. The world shrinks a bit when a waitress calls me "hon."

When my depression had augured to its most ominous depth, it was Trina who sat across the table from me in this very diner, sliding a tumbler of ice water my way and urging me to open the amber plastic prescription bottle and take my meds while she watched.

Trina has the easy social grace of a first lady, the mild philosophical nature and skinny arms of Kermit the Frog, and a tattoo of a sunflower on her right big toe. We don't remember how we first met, and we don't know how we lived without each other. Trina and I spoke over the phone; we know that much. She e-mailed me out of the blue for some military spouse–related reason. I e-mailed back, and we quickly moved to the telephone. Her husband, Antoine, was stationed in the South, and the guesthouse that Trina and Antoine were renting off the pool of a wealthy woman's estate had poor cellular reception, so we'd chat while she sat on the diving board.

No matter how much we talk about certain people being unflappable—and Trina, in my estimation, fits that bill—you can count on them being, um, *flapped* when religion comes up. Antoine's parents were, to put it politely, ambitiously fundamentalist Christian, ever proselytizing in a way that felt hostile and alienating to him, and their view created a great distance between parents and child. The word *Christian*, to Trina and Antoine, carried a certain connotation—or, I'll say it, stereotype—I was straining to work against. I was reluctant to wear a cross for that very reason: people with whom I was otherwise aligned might see it and assume the worst.

I call it the *Ned Flanders Effect*, named for Homer Simpson's dippy Holy Roller neighbor. Something about hearing that you identify as Christian moves people—otherwise good, reasonable, cultured people—to automatically start deducting your IQ points. A look comes over their faces: *Oh, crap, she's a pod person. She not going to start praying for me, is she? What if she's praying for me* right now?

I told Trina that I'd been reconnecting with my Christian roots. Her eyebrows raised so high, she could use them to dust the ceiling fans. Then the questions: What? Why? When?

I started to panic, imagining her deleting my number from her phone contacts right after breakfast. Jesus take the wheel, stat.

I cannot stand the idea of losing friends. I believe the diagnostic term for this condition is *codependent weenie*. Because I grew up feeling like a stranger in my own house, my friends became my chosen family—a tribe deeper than blood. When I felt exiled, I found shelter and uplift—to say nothing of places to live and things to eat and ways to make money—in their company.

I couldn't bear being rejected by Trina. It would be like the square-wheeled train being banished from the Island of Misfit Toys. (Though I suppose if I were a misfit toy, I'd be the Dolly for Sue, the baby doll who's always crying. According to the show's producer, Dolly considers herself a misfit due to her low self-esteem and psychological problems. Brokenness isn't always visible to the eye.)

Most of my friends—my unique, occasionally nuts, but wise, devoted, flung-far-and-wide friends—were raised with some sort of religious tradition that they later organically outgrew or hostilely rejected over time: Pentecostals who were threatened with damnation for watching "worldly" television shows like *Beverly Hills, 90210*; Jehovah's Witnesses who rebelled, writhing and screaming onstage in their art-rock bands as if they were demon-possessed; and recovering Catholics. So many recovering Catholics.

What had pulled them away from religion? Feminist frustration and disgust for entrenched sexism in the church. Feeling alienated and judged for being gay, bisexual, transgender, or even divorced. Seeing religion as justification for far too much violence, greed, and corruption, both past and present.

Atheism, agnosticism, and New Age spirituality, with their built-in call to self-sufficiency and personal responsibility, made much more sense to many of my friends. They aren't joiners. They are defectors, reformers, rebels, and Bartlebys who would really, when it came to organized religion, rather not. Their reasons were sound and not to be trifled with. If I wanted respect for the ways in which I felt directed, I needed to respect their direction too. I knew this fell outside the "one God above all" Christian evangelist tradition, but that was okay with me. I felt next to no missionary zeal.

Sometimes the only thing you can do is tell people the truth and hope they'll catch up to you.

You can't compare coming out Christian to coming out as gay. The stakes are inarguably lower, for one thing. Gay-bashing and discrimination are a known risk of coming out of the closet, but I've yet to hear of an American being met with violence for brandishing a Bible and saying, "Hey, guess what? Jesus rocks my world!" But neither is coming out as Christian as incidental as admitting you're a huge fan of, I don't know, scrapbooking. Or NASCAR. Still, there's a cultural connotation about observant Christians, a presumed thread of provincialism, with which one must contend and counter. So I wouldn't call it "coming out" so much as "coming forward."

Christians are having a bad moment in secular media—what with the prevalence of the irksome prosperity gospel that sounds like trickle-down economics with a Bible waved over it, combined with the ascension of a newfangled strain of Hipster Christian pastor—a tattooed dude in a fedora espousing the same old patriarchal interpretation of Scripture. Eve tempting Adam with the apple as man's downfall? Cool story, bro.

Bible-scarred friends like Trina's husband may assume I'm one of those people. I may also represent the dangerous territory from which they ran. Just how freaky of a Jesus freak are you? As your heart grows with the love of Christ, does your mind get smaller? These are not superficial concerns.

Trina, a precocious economist who earned her PhD by the age of thirty, is a warm and friendly version of a type who appears in my internal Greek chorus of critics: the educated, East Coast secular skeptic to whom organized religion is something you grow out of, not toward. A *truly* evolved person, says this critic, tosses off the life jacket and swims to freedom on her own. Self-sufficiency negates the needs of the spirit—an assessment both pat and topical enough to appear noncontroversial. I'd touted that line myself—Ayn Rand meets Malcolm Gladwell.

And there we were, Trina and I, on our second cups of tea. Her eyes were wide, incredulous, as she asked, "But what about the sexism? The antigay business?" I had flop sweat in the armpits of my pullover, and I struggled to explain progressive Christianity in a way that didn't disparage evangelicals or fundamentalists, though I may have used the words *cray-cray* and *completely insane*—in a loving, compassionate Christian way—when citing certain televangelist pastors. In explaining the more moderate, love-and-peace politics of my progressive ilk, I felt like Margaret Mead trying to describe the Trobriand Islanders.

Talk, they say, is cheap, but I've come to view it as priceless—the most direct route to understanding. Conversation, of course, is not the same as conversion. Rather, it is a two-way street containing multiple motivations and potential outcomes, and not every exchange will end with my feeling as if I've persuaded the person about my way of seeing. The nones may be having none of it, just as stalwart atheists may view me as that nice lady who believes in her imaginary friend, and more conservative Christians may see me as hopelessly flawed. (Well, aren't we all?) Still, after years of agnostic flailing, I can say with increasing certainty that there is hope, goodwill, and commitment to equality and justice as much in the name of Christ as in anything else, and now that I anticipate and understand the impetus behind the line of inquiry around that belief, I'm ready for the shakedown. More often than not, real conversation is an attempt to build a bridge, not a wall.

My omelet went cold and rubbery on my plate as I explained, feeling like the weakest kid on the freshman debate team. I didn't want to convert Trina; I simply wanted to connect. How sad, I thought, that the progressive, inclusive church has fallen so far from view that the prevailing assumption around Christianity is everything we're not.

Trina worked in local government with aspirations to run for office one day, and politics built the bridge I needed to get my point across. "I feel like if I don't help reclaim Christianity from the corrupting forces, then they win," I said. She understood my return to church when framed rhetorically: If you leave the church, to whom are you leaving it?

"Well," she said, as the waitress dropped the check, "if you're happy, then I'm happy for you!" Which seems more like something a friend would say after being introduced to your new, slightly dim boyfriend, but a win is a win, however small.

I grabbed the bill with a comedic flourish. "This one's on me, babydoll." Christian charity with jazz hands.

Occasionally, an old friend from the punk scene will jab an elbow in my ribs, tell me that this Jesus business is a silly turn of events, it's not at all what they'd have expected of me, and it's definitely not punk rock. I can't believe I'm still needled with "You're not a real punk!" accusations at this stage of my life. Is my soldier husband punk rock? Is my retirement fund? Iggy Pop songs are used for Cadillac commercials now. Twenty-five years ago, I'd have seen that as a huge affront and a sell-out. Now I think, *Well, if Iggy ever needs a hip replacement, maybe the royalties will help the old boy.* And anyway, I guess I'm still punk rock enough to say that if I'm not punk rock enough to meet somebody else's standards, too bad.

There is nothing punk rock about Jesus (though I suppose coming back from the dead after three days is pretty Goth); yet as incongruous as it seems, punk had been my salvation in more ways than one. First, the music saved my life; then, the ethos saved my soul. Punk edifies a curious nature that leads you to find an alternative to your given orthodoxies, and a story—and a place—for yourself that feels true. It led me from my family home to the East Village, then to San Francisco, and to points beyond. I couldn't have anticipated any of those moves any more than I could have anticipated ending up in church. But grace is surprising that way—it brings you places you never thought you'd go but somehow were always meant to be.

9

THE GLITTER HIGH

Over the past two years, I've lost more than a hundred pounds. There's nothing impressive about this feat. It's not as if I've lost the hundred-plus pounds sensibly, sequentially, and permanently. Rather, I've lost the same five pounds about twenty different times, thanks to a series of dubious dietary stunts.

Per the established metrics of weight-to-height ratio and body mass index, I'm not what a medical professional would call exceedingly overweight—though Hollywood, Madison Avenue, and the average "thinspiration" Pinterest page would post a dissenting opinion. Essentially, I'm your garden-variety mesomorph who doesn't eat to live but, rather, lives to eat her feelings.

What consumes me, urging me to mindlessly consume? Usually

nothing special. Like so many other people, I nosh my way through shame and regret about the past and anxiety about the future. But these depressive months were exceptionally tough—not only was my own mental health in tatters, but also my sister Kelly learned she had lupus; my husband's father was diagnosed with small-cell lung cancer; and my mother's breathing trouble landed her in the hospital repeatedly. It was not a good couple of years for illusions of familial immortality.

No.

All my adult life, no matter what I ate or how much, I could always count on peeling off five pounds in a few days by drinking lemon water sprinkled with cayenne pepper, tossing back a couple of health store herbal diuretics, and shunning gluten, sugar, and dairy. Then I'd get stressed and close out my evenings by pulling into a fast-food parking lot to eat a jumbo drive-through value meal away from the shaming glow of streetlamps, only to go back on my regimen of water, diuretics, and selective privation. Then, during the long roll-out of bad family news, the stress eating became a constant and the weight came on and stayed.

In the midst of all the awfulness, I received a tremendous gift: a namesake dress. My friend Laura, whom I've known since the days of the CBGB Sunday hardcore matinees, built a thriving clothing business based on her original designs inspired by vintage '40s and '50s silhouettes. Her line, Pinup Girl Clothing, features an adorable array of va-va-voomy dresses, and she'd designed one to my specifications—a body-skimming sheath with day-to-night versatility, made of stretchy fabric with a neckline that's not too low, a hemline that's not too high, and longish sleeves. I was looking for two specific features: forgiveness and good coverage.

As soon as it came off the production line, the Burana dress was delivered to me in every available color—black, navy, plum, and green tea. I zipped myself into the navy, then turned and turned before the mirror. *Look at this tailoring,* I thought. *Gorgeous, gorgeous, gorgeous.* My next thought: *Oh man, I am way too fat to wear this.* I could have asked Laura to send me a bigger size—Pinup Girl sizes items from XS to 2X. But no, I decided, I would wait until I was thin enough to feel good in the dresses I had.

Waiting to feel good was an elusive proposition, physically, emotionally, and spiritually. In search of comfort beyond the edible realm, I started digging deeper into my quest for some sort of godlike sustenance. I went to yoga more regularly and read books on snuggly, big-tent, lefty Christianity, Buddhism, radical acceptance, being in the now. None of it felt better than two double cheeseburgers with extra mustard and large fries washed down by a bucket of Diet Coke, but it seemed important to at least be on the hunt for a more enduring means of soothing my feelings of guilt, loss, and vulnerability. I wanted a sense that I was okay, as a bulwark against life's slights. I wanted both forgiveness and good coverage. Is it strange that I wanted the same things from a dress as I did from God?

Then the next box arrived, packed full of more dresses by Laura and her design partner: the crazy orange-tiger Vamp; the demure yellow-rose-print Erika; the berry, blue, and red siren-sleek Erin; the luxe mauve velvet Mon Cheri with the draped cowl neckline; and the full-skirted cherry-print Heidi, which put me in a good mood just looking at it. They fit. Barely. One hardy sneeze and I'd bust the seams.

On the same day came an invitation to judge the Miss Exotic World competition at the Burlesque Hall of Fame Weekend in Las Vegas, only a few weeks away in early June. My friend Jo, whom I had long considered a sister in leopard print, was an event organizer, and she needed one more vintage-style enthusiast to round out the panel of judges. She knew I loved the playful, flamboyant *boom-shaka-laka* of old-school burlesque.

Why not? I thought. All the reading I'd been doing featured women coming to terms with the chaos of their lives by scaling back, mellowing out, making gratitude lists, cooking up pots of homemade lentil soup while wearing comfortable sweats, or—on the more moneyed side of spiritual seeking—jetting off to some guru in Belize for a silent meditation retreat. But I didn't want any kind of retreat. I didn't want to retreat, period. I had been hidden for so long in sadness. I wanted to surge forward, back into the electric stream of life. A couple of days in a flashy, sequin-saturated environment might be balm for my girly-girl soul.

I scored a cheap coach-class ticket and jammed my full Pinup Girl kit into my roll-aboard suitcase, along with four pairs of platform shoes, three pairs of false eyelashes, a waist-length hairpiece, a small heap of rhinestone jewelry, and twenty clip-in hair flowers— the spoils of eBay bargain hunting. Like a good Christian woman, I tossed a strapless push-up bra into the suitcase as well. I sipped a Diet Coke on the flight—the contest was twelve hours away. Could I lose enough water weight in time to really fit into the dresses? And wouldn't I feel fabulous if I did—as if I had some control over things? Wouldn't that be a nice change of course? I had been doing the hard work of facing my problems, and now I just wanted a big, tacky break from it all.

Dressing for the contest was an exercise in holding my breath and minding my worst thoughts with discipline and compassion: *Blah* feel fat *blah blah blah. Blah blah* lose ten more pounds *blah blah.* "It is what it is," I said aloud to my reflection. As I layered my makeup, I realized that so much of this "being present" business is simply telling the negative voices in your head to shut the heck up.

I pulled out a red dress with side shirring and lots of stretch. The perfect choice. A red dress says, "I'm here." My world is falling apart around me, with illness and whispers of decline at every turn, but I'm here.

Sometimes, despite all the acceptance and gentle-eyed self-appraisal, you put on your best tight-as-you-dare dress to find—discouragingly, irrefutably—that your rump looks like two hams rumbling in a sack. Here's the mindful, radically accepting solution: wear a fuller skirt. Or, if you simply can't stand the view, surrender to Spanx. They make lovely, center-squeezing, cellulite-smoothing fishnet tights. Mind the metaphor: If you feel like you're exploding in all kinds of uncomfortable directions, there's a multibillion-dollar industry built around helping you hold it together. Just roll them on, get over yourself, and get to the party. The goal weight—and the water pills and the rice cakes and the Pilates classes—will be there to-morrow. And the next day . . . and the next. Recapturing your ideal form doesn't have to slide from the wish list. Acceptance is not the same as settling—it's simply giving your impossible expectations the evening off.

A cloud of hairspray, a red rose pinned into my bouffant, and six-inch scarlet sequined pumps later, I was cruising through the casino looking like a one-woman prison riot.

I was the shrinking violet in this crowd, though. Satin, corsets, cleavage, high femme fabulosity, butch drag, and gender bending—everyone was bringing it like this was Prom Night of the Damned. Two female dandies in bespoke suits sat as if on princely thrones, hav-ing their wingtips polished by the casino shoeshine; every curvy girl was serving bodycon eveningwear as if it were her personal mission.

The hairdos and hats were so tall that the event organizers established a height rule for the showroom. One girl wore a yellow dress with a tutu skirt and a Swarovski crystal–bedazzled rubber duck on her head. We were the beautiful people not because we were so naturally blessed but because we put in the time. God said, "Let there be light," and we beamed it out to the universe in all our radiant, geeky glory—wild, weird, and holy too.

The show was exquisite—hour upon hour and act upon act of retro-styled pleasure. Unlike strip clubs, where appeasing the customer ego and libido drives the dynamic, a burlesque show is pure self-expression and delight. Campy, sophisticated, funny, clever, dear—what a thrill to see sexy performance for pleasure, instead of a grind for daily bread. Women wrapped in pink flamingo boas, men in bowler hats and booty shorts. This was equal opportunity objectification, with fun as the bottom line. The performers came from every corner of the world—Australia, Italy, Japan—and Salome smiled upon them all from behind her seven veils.

After the contest ended and the winners were chosen, I retired to the casino's TGI Fridays with the rest of the glittered rabble and ate the world's greasiest quesadilla while watching the merrymakers stream by on the way to the after-party. By the time I headed up to my room, it was five a.m.—eight a.m. if we're adjusting for time zones. I doffed my wig, scrubbed off my makeup, and lowered into bed, feeling satisfied and fully alive. I was glowing inside. In the burlesque world, it's called "the glitter high." I got it. Sometimes you just need to get into that full-femme battle rattle and ride the night down to its pathetic, wheezing last. The grave can wait and so, for that matter, can sleep.

I woke three hours later, pupils pinned in the beam of Vegas morning sunlight that streamed through the cheap hotel blinds, totally alert and not ravenously hungry for the first time in months, reborn in the Temple of Glitz. At the bathroom sink, I thought of Ram Dass: "Treat everyone you meet like God in drag."[1] Then I steepled my fingers and did a grateful little bow with my toothbrush.

I had seen beauty in the dark in its most florid manifestation; and in the fakery, some mojo I'd been missing was restored. In the fight for spiritual life, joy is the weapon of choice.

Today, as on most days, I opened the closet and ran my hands across the row of Pinup Girl dresses, thinking, *Okay, cartoony paradigm of feminine appearance, I've given you enough. It's boots and jeans again today. I'm shrinking back to my workaday DEFCON Level 5 femme. The burly-q swag and the war paint can wait.*

But they won't wait for long, because I can now clearly see that there will come a time when the riotous red-dress occasions are overtaken in quantity by somber black-dress ceremonies.

Back in the days of my pious punk youth, Saint Ian of Fugazi sang that "you can't be what you were, so you better start being just what you are." While I never forgot those words, I didn't really act on them until recently. Now I felt a sense of urgency as I returned to the sentiment again and again, like a mantra or a prayer. Carpe diem, carpe dazzle. Big or little, at our ideal size or far from it, this is the only show we get, no turning back.

There is a spirituality to every kind of theater, and what, I ask you, is more theatrical than a woman doing her best to work it? Costume, makeup, inhabiting a role so thoroughly that you're transformed by it—it's all there. God's loving acceptance is a come-as-you-are proposition, but it's my secretly held belief that every time you step out in something a little flashy, a million glittery angels chorus a resounding, "Yes!" Then you peel off the false lashes, get back into your jeans and boots or yoga pants, and roll onward, refreshed and inspired by the knowledge that somewhere between God and glamour, grace prevails.

Slip the red dress from the hanger. Tuck the silk flower behind your ear. Hide the scale and head out the door. The rest of your one-and-only life is waiting.

I will if you will.

Let's go.

10

STEPMONSTER

I guarantee that no pint-size princess, dreaming about a future of bridal gowns, wedding cakes, and happily-ever-after bliss, has wistfully, wishfully, said, "When I grow up, I want to marry a handsome prince who's been married before and has two kids."

I became a stepmother when I married Mike, father of two sons, Chris and Mikey, ages eight and ten. The morning I first met the boys, when Mike and I were still dating, we picked them up at his mother Mary's house in Rhinebeck for a day together at the Dutchess County Fair. I fretted in the passenger seat of Mike's dark green SUV as we pulled into the driveway. Would they like me? If Mike and I married, would I be stepmother material?

"Don't do all your worrying in advance," Mike said.

I flipped down the sun visor mirror and pawed through my purse for my makeup bag, a lipstick-seeking missile. "Do you even know who I am?"

I was already worrying about how weird it would be to have a queue for the mother-of-the-groom dances at the boys' weddings. Is there a separate stepmother-of-the-groom dance? Do their mother and I wear coordinating dresses? Who hosts the rehearsal dinner? Do we both get called "Nana" when the grandbabies come? How does this even work?

Sitting together on the plaid armchair in Mary's den, Mikey and Chris seemed unbearably little, though they were both tall for grammar schoolers. Handsome, both with hair cropped short, they were unmistakably brothers, though Mikey was reserved and pensive, his large brown eyes brooding under heavy brows, while Chris was talkative and curious, with fairer coloring, his eyes a cool speckled grey.

The earthy scent of warm hay wafted from the 4-H barns as we wound our way through the humid fairway. There were ring-toss game booths stuffed with toys, carts selling candy apples, and people carrying fried dough that sizzled on paper plates under snowy drifts of powdered sugar. Mike and I waited on the ground as the boys spun and plunged through the air on carnival rides that made us nauseated just watching. The four of us sat on a bench and shared a plastic bucket of French fries, then I treated them to ice cream, the classic move of a knock-kneed performer auditioning for a high-stakes audience of prospective family. I would love to know exactly how many tons of white sugar have gone into building these connections.

It's not easy to reshape a family around a broken marriage, no matter how committed everyone is to keeping the peace. A second marriage represents a new beginning, but it also sinks a headstone atop the previous union. Even if kids know rationally that their parents won't reunite, it's not reasonable to expect them to receive a reminder of this gladly, which makes things awkward when that reminder is you.

The primary question that faced me as a stepmother felt very confusing, but at its core it was clear: What do I *do*, exactly? When you're a mother, the role is sharply defined: Keep the child clean, warm, safe, dry, and fed, then, also, later on, educated, guided to a moral existence, and possibly discouraged from buying seven pairs of shoes or a Fender Strat with those first paychecks. Liking them is assumed; loving them a must. If there's a mother already at the helm of the *Enterprise* on that mission when you marry a man with children, how do you fit in? Are you just some redshirt roaming the periphery of the ship, superfluous until death?

The Bible lends no wisdom particular to the task of stepparenting. Abraham was Sarah's second husband, and Joseph was Jesus' stepfather, really—his father being God himself. (You know *that* marriage had to have some awkward moments.) But role models are nearly nonexistent. So where do you turn? Disney? Per the stories born in the Magic Kingdom, the chief requirements of stepmothering appear to be consuming vanity, sabotage, and possibly dispensing poison apples.

In the years since I met the boys and married their father, I have done much to make the special days really special—*We're going to create precious holiday memories, dammit!*—with many missteps along the way. Among them, the Valentine's Day when I baked them brownies decorated with chocolate hearts melting and gooey on the surface. The boys hovered over the warm baking pan, plates up, as I promised to cut them big pieces. Butter knife in hand, I said, "But before I give you a brownie, tell me," my voice ascending into a singsong so pathetic I cringed as I heard it, "will you be my valentines?" (So needy.) When they were fourteen and twelve, respectively, I gave them beautifully gift-wrapped organic zit serum in their Christmas stockings. (Seriously.)

Stepping into the role of proxy *mater* is awkward, as we expect so much from mothers: effortless emotional intimacy and a knack for anticipating needs while enforcing discipline in a firm but lovable manner. That's a pretty big burrito to have shoved your way. Add to that, if the children's mother is still in the picture, the stepmother is never to usurp her authority. The perennial good sport, the stepmother must step back to honor birth mom's primacy, but step forward when her help is needed. (Step back, step forward—is this what makes you a "step" mother? How am I only realizing this now?) The ideal stepmother fully and gratefully inhabits her role, but also knows her place. The ambiguity is taxing. I haven't checked the rate of incidence of stress-induced hypertension in stepmothers, but perhaps I should.

Somehow I got it into my head that second wife equaled second place, so overcompensation became my hobby. I tried for so long to be a model stepmom—mild-mannered, fun, lighthearted, relentlessly understanding, self-sacrificing, and ever ready to put my own needs second, even in my own house when they came for weekend visits. The boys and I always got along great. The only complication was that I was exhausted and resentful from being so fake all the time—the circus ringmaster trotting out jokes, personalized birthday cakes, and frozen pizzas. Years passed, and every other weekend and two weeks during summer break I still felt as if I were in the audition phase, like an awkward, repeating series of first dates. I had an unrelenting need to know that I'd made the cut. "What other people think of me is none of my business," said no stepmother ever.

I didn't consciously drop my mask; it fell off by accident. The boys were sixteen and fourteen at the time. They were over for a visit, and I whacked my head on the overhang coming down the tiny, narrow staircase in our little old Victorian house. The boys could hear my melon make contact with a loud crack from where they sat in the living room playing video games. My hands flew to my forehead. "If I hit my [expletive] head on this [expletive] overhang one more [expletive] time," I yelled, "I'm moving to a [expletive] hotel!"

Well. Guess I showed them what a role model really is.

The boys were both confirmed Catholic, but in their late teens—those years of rebellion and questioning and thinking it's okay to wear knit caps to the dinner table—they leaned toward atheism, which went over like a lead balloon with their father. They tried flexing their debating muscles with him, but they were outmatched—the man had decades of experience, and he could drop a C. S. Lewis quote like a neutron bomb. There was one Thanksgiving dinner when the two Mikes went at it over the existence of God so strenuously, all the other guests left the table one by one until we were clustered in the kitchen, watching in disbelief through the pass-through window as father and son verbally duked it out. I was so afraid of rocking the boat, I didn't dare say, "Hey, you two, could you cut it out? Your mother cooked all morning, everybody is hungry, and the gravy's getting cold!" There's an old saying that goes, "If you think you're enlightened, spend a week with your family." Though in many cases, a single holiday will do.

I didn't know what the boys' mother thought about their atheism, or how she responded to it. But in this case, I felt my way swiftly to my role. My job was to respect the boys' independent thinking, to tell them what I believed (that there was a supreme being; that I didn't respect them less for disagreeing; that I hoped they'd remain open to changing their minds), and then to stay out of it.

Mike's father was recovering from surgery to remove a cancerous tumor in his lung when we brought the boys down to his house in Queens—a three-story Archie Bunker multiunit on a quiet street in Woodhaven. His wife, Lucia—my stepmother-in-law—welcomed us via the back door, through the small kitchen and into the dining room. Lucia is only ten years older than me. Since she married into the family when Mike and his younger sister were teenagers, they have always called her "Azia" (Italian for *aunt*), but I call her my "hot mama."

Eight people sat around the table, their relationship to each other all crisscrossed lines diagrammed on a whiteboard: a couple of second wives, a half-brother and sister, two brothers, two full brother-sister combinations, plus two dogs, one big, one little. A healthy mix, a thoroughly modern family. Lucia hadn't had time to make one of her grand feasts after work, so when the doorbell rang, pizza boxes were brought in from the hallway and stacked four-high—two sausage, a pepperoni, an extra cheese. As someone who views pizza delivery as one of the hallmarks of civilization, I was more than happy with this Sunday dinner. Lucia passed around paper plates, then set out a shaker of red pepper flakes and a canister of grated Parmesan to top our slices.

Sated, we sat groaning around the dining room table, which was covered in a goldenrod brocade satin cloth, as the plates were gathered up and tossed out. Hot Mama and I drank red wine and Diet

Coke from juice glasses. The back of my chair bumped the cherry wood curio cabinet crowded with porcelain figurines and Yankees memorabilia—a waltzing girl in a swirling ball gown next to an autographed Joe DiMaggio baseball. Mike's baby sister, Jennifer, born when he was seventeen, was now thirty-one and about to get married to a rugged Irish firefighter.

We admired Jennifer's engagement ring, which made me think of Mike's mother, Mary, who had, that past Christmas, surprised me by giving me her own mother's engagement ring from her second husband, Sal. Sal worked as a barber, and he had designed the ring himself—a showy, white gold Rat Pack sparkler with a beautifully cut round center stone surrounded by a fan of tiny leaves dotted with melee diamonds. A grand gesture of sacrifice from a humble man to his beautician bride, who had singlehandedly raised her son and daughter in an apartment alongside the raised track of the J train on Jamaica Avenue. As I turned the ring this way and that so the stones sparkled in the light, there was nothing I could say except a whispered thank you. The ring, in being passed to me, said: *You belong to us. Family.*

The conversation at the Sunday dinner table in Queens turned from Jennifer's ring to her dress—a strapless fishtail gown with lace overlay and a crystal-buckled belt that would encircle her tiny waist—to the wedding mass at the local parish. Talk shifted to memories of Mike and me marrying at Baltimore City Hall, a quickie civil ceremony prior to his last deployment. We'd planned to have a formal wedding at West Point later on, but my father died four months before the wedding, and, as I told Mike's family, I couldn't stand the idea of not having someone to walk me down the aisle.

Mikey piped up. "I would have walked you down the aisle."

Every so often, a person will spontaneously say something that means more than a million scripted sentiments ever could. My insides immediately went to Jell-O as years of doubt crumpled inside me. I thought I knew speechless when my mother-in-law gave me her mother's diamond ring. I didn't.

My eyes stung with tears, and I held out my hands to Mikey, as if I might hug him, but my arms hung in the air and I made a pathetic little "meep" sound like Beaker from *The Muppet Show*. When you marry into a blended family, being included in the lineup of adults is so lovely, but acceptance from the kids means the most. Little moments tell the larger tale. Family isn't always blood. Family is a feeling. A sense of ease and comfort and understanding that you are seen, cared for, and appreciated, even the bizarre parts. Especially the bizarre parts.

The enchanted family love bubble popped when we were getting ready to return home. We specialize in the Italian Good-bye, where leaving a family gathering takes almost as much time as the get-together itself for all the farewell kissing and hugging and promising future meetings. Sodas for the road and foil-wrapped food are proffered as parting gifts. The last one out the door might escape without a bag of leftovers and cookies pressed into their hands.

The boys and I loaded into Mike's car, then I hopped out when I realized I'd forgotten my purse inside. I happened to be standing in the best place in the driveway to take a shot of wiper fluid right in the eye when it arced over the top of the car after Mike decided to hit the button to clear the windshield for the ride home. Once again, the boys were treated to my cursing, sputtering self. If I aim to be reliable as a stepmother, I will never let them down in this regard at least.

Being a stepmother—the kind who doesn't go around dispensing poison apples at snack time—requires a generosity of heart that is rarely acknowledged. The word *thankless* might occasionally spring to mind. You don't want a cookie or a gold star; you merely want to know that you mattered, and that you were, at least every so often, appreciated—if not for your contribution to the family firmament, then for your flexibility and good nature and maybe those Sunday morning scrambled eggs you hustled to make instead of shoving cold cereal everyone's way when they stumbled into the kitchen, finally awake at noon.

But, as it often does, the work of gratitude and appreciation falls to the person seeking it, and the reward shows up in flashes more than in broad statements or gestures. The little things, as they say. When the boys where fifteen and thirteen, we took a Sunday afternoon drive with their dad and our dog down to Little Stony Point, a park on the Hudson with a narrow, sandy swimming beach. We were united in our love for the dog—a big yellow Labrador named Chief, whom we'd adopted off the West Point bulletin board when his owner had to surrender him. We walked the winding dirt path knuckled with tree roots as the dog bounded ahead to the beachfront.

Chief was the Big Lebowski with fur. He saw a white bleach bottle way out in the water repurposed as a buoy and swam toward it as we tried, uselessly, to call him back. The early spring wind whipped the water's surface into white peaks, the speed and strength of the current visible in the flotsam of leaves and sticks bobbing downriver. The four of us hollered for the dog to return, but he kept on paddling until we were worried he would become exhausted and get swept away.

He turned around eventually, abandoning his retrieval project, and swam back to shore, where we lavished him with head pats and a scrub-down with an old towel. Then we knocked around in the pebbly sand, and I took photos of my four boys. In the excitement, I didn't have extra energy to feel excluded or out of plumb. Pets have that magic ability to pull you out of yourself and into the present: muddy paws, snuffly noses, and raised adrenaline.

On the ride home, "Sweet Child of Mine" came on the radio, and Mikey and Chris began singing along. For a couple of kids born in the nineties, they knew a surprising number of eighties radio hits. I joined in, yowling with Axl Rose as he pitched into his feline falsetto. Mike kept his eyes on the road, hands steady on the wheel. Axl sang, "Where do we go now?" The answer was nowhere but here. Here was the best possible place—dirty car upholstery, wet dog smell, and all.

Joy is happiness without the hardship edited out, and these boys taught me how to break down joy and love into singular moments. If stepmothering feels at times like a can't-win situation, it helps to remember that winning is never the point of love anyway. The most significant thing that being their stepmother has taught me is that if you're waiting for things to be perfect to be grateful, don't.

The spiritual lesson of stepmothering is adaptability—honoring the primal loyalty between mother and child while being true to your own strange and needy self; turning the other cheek while doling out a hug to a kid who's somehow, suddenly, a full head taller than you. For me, being a stepmother isn't about inhabiting a role that absorbs as much spotlight as a capital-*M* Mom, or stepping into a primary gig as parent. It's about knowing that the role will be elusive at the start and shift over time. It's about having the humor and resilience to handle life on life's terms, even when reality is so far from a fairy tale that you fantasize about running away to work as a truck stop waitress in Arizona under an assumed identity. It's about collecting funny, sentimental, and warm moments one at a time until you have a loosely assembled memory book with so many pages it catches you by surprise. Like getting to know God, or yourself, it's about the long game.

It's about singing along to the radio on a cloudy Sunday, sounding pretty terrible but feeling pretty great, with two boys, neither one a sweet child of mine, but each very much a child of my heart.

11

THIS IS MY BODY

I nearly died in childbirth. Twice.

Two days before Easter 2014, thirty-two weeks into my otherwise normal pregnancy, I went in to the Army hospital for a checkup. My OB-GYN, Dr. Yavorek, a civilian with waist-length hippie hair and toes that peeked out from Birkenstocks with a perfect pedicure in a crazy color, noticed a concerning spike in both my weight and my blood pressure. The numbers weren't high, she said, but they were high for me. I trusted she wasn't being overly cautious or dramatic; thus far she'd been a steadfast and reassuring physician.

No chocolate bunnies, pastel eggs, or lily-perfumed "He Is Risen" church service for me the following day. I spent Easter Sunday with an Omron blood pressure cuff velcroed around my wrist and knee-high black nylon compression socks squeezing my ever-swelling ankles, my feet propped up on the arm of the living room couch, elevated above my heart.

Almost eight months earlier, when I looked down and saw, after months of negative at-home pregnancy tests, that the digital readout said "Pregnant," I jolted alert. It was four thirty in the morning, and I'd grabbed the stick reflexively as I headed into the bathroom, fully expecting another negative. There is a down-the-rabbit-hole feeling of seeing a positive pregnancy test. A million future possibilities explode at once in a psychedelic burst as the edges of your current life start to melt and curl in on themselves. I stared, so used to seeing a single pink line where there should be two, sure my bleary eyes were deceiving me.

Mike was still asleep, his form mounded like a friendly hibernating bear beneath the comforter, the pillows cradling his head. Given the hour, I thought the kind thing would be to let him sleep a little longer.

I couldn't wait.

I shook him awake. "Mike! Mike! I'm pregnant!"

Over the weeks I was happy, then nauseated, then strafed by heartburn that made the sight of food terrifying. But by some miracle, the hormonal stew of pregnancy bathed my brain in oxytocin, my depression calmed, and I was serene as a Maalox-clutching Buddha. The blissful cotton-roll fog cosseting my brain made it easy to leave off the antidepressants for the duration of my pregnancy.

But now there was potential trouble on the horizon. As I sat in the car after the doctor's appointment, I said a prayer. Turns out I'm not a down-on-your-knees praying type; I find myself reaching out to God anyplace I'm prone to rumination. Waiting rooms, at the sink doing dishes, in bed at night when I'm seeking an alternative to the endless internal stream of fretful chatter. And on this day, in a hospital parking lot in the front seat of a Subaru.

Martin Luther said to pray and let God worry, but I find I do both by turns, with the hope that my prayers may at least be propelled by that fretful energy into the proper hands. At the outset of my pregnancy, Dr. Yavorek, unfazed by my "advanced maternal age," refrained from declaring me high-risk. However, she said, should I go into labor early, I might have to deliver at another hospital, one better equipped with a NICU. I was emotionally invested in the baby being born at West Point. Since Mike and I were stationed there in 2003, the place had become dear to me: I knew its history and the contours of its hilly geography. When Mike retired after twenty years of military service, his ceremony was held in West Point's Pershing Hall, under the forbidding oil portrait gaze of old BlackJack himself. Though Mike and I no longer reside on post, a piece of our shared heart does. For me, having the baby at Keller qualified as a home birth.

Six Sundays after Easter, I was back at West Point for another checkup. Holding onto Mike's arm, I was so bloated I practically sloshed into the hospital. I could barely cram my swollen feet into my old Nikes. Dr. Yavorek was off for the weekend, and Dr. November was the attending. I'd seen him once before for a routine vitals check, and appreciated that his camouflage scrubs were complemented by a camouflage yarmulke.

After an ultrasound revealed that the baby was healthy, he informed me that I had preeclampsia and was at very high risk of stroke or seizure. "So," he said, clapping his hands together, "the way you cure preeclampsia is to deliver the baby. Would you like to have a baby today? Maybe tomorrow?"

"No, thank you," I said brightly. But, I told him, I'd be happy to come back in two weeks on my due date.

Dr. November looked at Mike. "Do you have her bag in the car?"

I agreed to try inducing labor the following morning, since the baby wasn't in distress. But after six hours, each second counted out in drops of Pitocin, my blood pressure continued creeping up. Dr. November came in to check my cervix, all yuks and smiles. He poked and prodded, exclaiming, "See, now that's pathetic! You're not dilated at all!" The Army's answer to Patch Adams had spoken. It was showtime.

At three p.m. sharp, I was wheeled down the hall to the operating room for an emergency Cesarean. Dr. Yavorek, in her scrubs, said hello, and I could see her eyes smiling over her surgical mask as she joined Dr. November next to the operating table. I considered it my patriotic duty to let all the young Army medics in the room stay to observe, even though there were so many of them bustling about, it felt as though I was giving birth during a Knicks game.

What a C-section birth lacks in organic high, it makes up for in expedience. No pushing or straining, and no pain. Thirty-nine minutes later, my daughter was born rosy, robust, and squalling. Mike later told me that I was smiling the entire time. The surgical assistant called out, "Here's your daughter!" as Dr. Yavorek swung her little body up so I could get a peek at her over the curtain that concealed the surgical site. Then they whisked her away for cleaning, weighing, foot-printing— the classic "Welcome to Planet Earth" delivery room ritual.

All throughout my pregnancy, or at least once I was far enough along that I was convinced the pregnancy would stick, I had worried—because I always worry—that when I met my daughter, she might seem alien to me, that I'd feel no immediate connection. I knew this was a normal way of giving birth, but I still wanted that *whoosh* of love at first sight. When they brought her over to me, scrubbed up and swaddled, I took one look at her self-possessed little face, an arc of long dark lashes curving from each crimped-closed eyelid, and I was a goner. She was crying, and as the nurse held her down close to my face so Mike and I could nuzzle her, I said, "Hi! Hi!" and she stopped crying at the sound of my voice.

I not only loved her with a force that could crush a planet; I felt a seismic shift inside of me—a grounding, as if I had been reintroduced to some primitive core self. For everything that had hurt me or caused me fear and suspicion and doubt, I had made it through to this. She was here. She was healthy. She was beautiful. She was ours, for good, and places in me that had been shattered fused to whole. My child healed my heart.

The physician's assistant congratulated me and then said, "Dr. Yavorek is almost done with you, then we'll take you to recovery." And I'll never forget this, as he glanced at the hanging sheet that spared me the view. "We just have to put everything back in."

During the standard post-op exam, Mike stood at the head of the recovery room bed, feeding me ice chips from a plastic spoon. As the nurse palpated my belly, I felt a horrific gush, went cold all over, and my teeth started chattering. I heard my voice, small as if pulsing in from a distant star, "I think I'm bleeding more than I'm supposed to."

From there, the room went black. I would not know until two days later that I'd had a massive hemorrhage that proved fearsomely difficult to contain. Had it gone on much longer, I would have lost either my uterus or my life.

During the hemorrhage and the hours after, I drifted in and out of consciousness, not sure whether or not I was imagining the troop of nurses, the doctors I didn't recognize, and the chief of staff of the hospital, hovering around my bed. Everyone had gathered trying to figure out what to do to stop the hemorrhaging. Needles stabbed the veins in the back of my hands, the side of my wrist.

In my darkest hallucinating hour, Mother Mary didn't come to me. Instead, it was Dr. November in his sweaty gym shorts, T-shirt, and yarmulke, paged to return to the hospital in the middle of his softball practice, swiftly and calmly injecting syringes of oxytocin into my hip flesh to stop the bleed-out. No jokes this time, only a worried expression and medical diligence. A nurse, magically named Teresa, kept vigil by my bed the entire night, administering transfusions and covering me in blankets from the warming cupboard. I'd come to now and then, and she'd assure me that she would be by my side every second, no matter what. I remember very little, but I do recall a perfectly lucid moment of gratitude for everyone who had ever donated blood.

When my blood pressure stayed dangerously high over the following days, necessitating drugs that counter-indicated breastfeeding—that Holy Grail of conscientious motherhood—I didn't see Jesus. Nor was I visited by a seraph with a harp and flowing golden curls. Instead, the nurses sat holding the baby in the nursery and brought her in to me every few hours, placing her in my arms so I could feed her the tiniest little bottles of formula. I asked them to take me off the magnesium sulfate drip as soon as possible so I could try breast-feeding my daughter, but she couldn't get the hang of it. The nurses unswaddled my baby and stripped her down to her diaper, so she'd huddle in close to me seeking skin-on-skin warmth. I tried cradling her to my breast, then tucking her under my arm like a football, but all she would do was scream and cry, her whole shivering body turning bright red. This of course made *me* cry too. Over four work shifts, eight different women tried to help the baby latch. Good nurses are angels on earth.

Dr. Yavorek told me they'd do everything they could to help me breastfeed, but giving a bottle wasn't the worst thing. "All five kids in my family were formula-fed," she told me, "and we all grew up to be doctors."

Standing for the first time after the C-section was more painful than the surgery itself. With a nurse on either side of me gripping me by my elbows, I pushed myself up from the side of the bed, bent forward as though I'd rusted over at the hips. Then I tried straightening up, grotesque scarlet whorls of cramping pain radiating up, down, and outward from my center. My midsection and my thighs felt like one big charley horse. I must've looked like the guy in Edvard Munch's *The Scream* as I creaked and moaned my way up to fully vertical. I caught sight of my bloated legs, which looked, from thigh to ankle, like fish-belly white tree trunks. *Is this my body now?*

I shuffled, in baby Frankenstein steps, to the bathroom for my first shower. Stripping down before the bathroom mirror, I still looked hugely pregnant in my hospital-issue mesh granny panties. I edged into the shower stall. Holding on to the metal handrail, I examined my belly with tender curiosity. The incision was taped together over the internal stitches, vertical adhesive slashes along the curve, a Jack Skellington smile on my flesh. *This* is *my body now.* As I soaped the row of tape strips carefully, I thought about those celebrity mommy photos, where the mom snaps back mere days after delivery, and within weeks is in a bikini, frolicking on the beach at St. Barts with nary a stretch mark. One in three births in America is a C-section. How great would it be to see a celebrity with a scar emerging from the surf? Aphrodite with some miles on her.

I rinsed off and patted my belly down with the rough, postage stamp hospital towel, certain that the first famous mom who shows up on the beach in a tiny thong-bottom bikini that rides below her fully visible scar would be elevated to goddess status. So many women, scared and opened up on a table and stitched together afterward, would feel validated. My incision, over time, would heal crookedly, fading to the palest lavender. Being a mother was something no one could ever take from me. So, too, this scar.

During the weeklong recovery, Mike roomed with me in the foldout easy chair next to my bed. I'd always been moved by his stalwart faith, but as HGTV flickered in the dark, he said, quietly, "While they were working on you, I told God if you died, that was *it* for me."

I didn't think less of him for his confession. I knew from experience that shaking your fist at God is its own form of praying—at least the line of communication is still open. If God's love is unconditional, then I figure that good, clean rage is as welcome as swooning submission. Honesty is the only rule of prayer.

Despite a birth that had gone wrong, my new baby sleeping not in my arms but alone in the nursery so I could rest, and a husband tossing fitfully on the floor of my hospital room beside me, I was grateful to have what was starting to feel like a reliable connection to God. I wasn't worried about my daughter. I trusted my sense that she would be fine, even though we were forced apart. Even if things went bad again and I had the stroke the doctors feared. Call it the voice of God or the first whisper of mother's intuition, but something told me we would be okay. I think they call it faith. After all, what is faith but hope with field experience?

Eventually, my blood pressure dropped out of critical range and I was cleared to go home. Mike pushed me out of the labor and delivery wing in a wheelchair. I wore bright yellow hospital socks with the nonskid bottoms since my feet were too swollen to fit into my shoes. He wheeled me out the hospital's sliding glass doors, bundled up with my painkillers, my disappointment, my joy, and our dark-haired baby girl. Before Mike gingerly clicked the baby's car carrier into the backseat, a passing soldier took our photo. Our family first. As we drove away, the ugly, blocky hospital building looked as holy as a shrine. But no random floating miracle had occurred there; modern medicine had saved my life. Grace was just the attendant.

With my daughter, and with God, in my life, I'm still the same broken, neurotic mess I always was. And that's okay, because these are relationships I'll have for life, and beyond. That's the miracle of grace, one that keeps even skeptics like me entranced by the promise of Easter. We fall, we suffer, and things land so distressingly far afield of where we'd wanted, but—as I learned from Reverend Kim—pain is not the end of the story. We get a second shot, we rise again. Scarred and restored, I wouldn't compare myself to Jesus. I knew better. (Not to mention, that didn't work out too well for the Beatles.) But I do know that the story of his rebirth is my story, our story. Knowing that we are connected to something huge and loving and eternal, we can endure the ways in which we are pained, and then, delivered, marvel at the scars we've got to show for it. We can, as Flannery O'Connor once said, "with one eye squinted take it all as a blessing."[1]

12

THE ISLE OF MOM

Sometimes I think that the contented, roseate glow of new mother-hood is humanity's most egregious case of false advertising. Under every soft-focus stock photo of a blissed-out, showered, and well-groomed mother beaming down at her adorable newborn baby, there should be a caption that reads, "This may be the loneliest you will ever feel."

If it were up to me, baby manuals would be required by law to contain a chapter called, "The First Ninety Days: Baby Thunderdome," with every directly-to-the-point word written in thirty-point bold type, with terms like *isolation, sleep deprivation, anxiety,* and *marital tension* underlined for emphasis. The opening paragraph would read: "The first ninety days are a hurricane of wild, wild love and insane adjustment as you try to figure out the kid's needs and rhythms. (If they have rhythms. Some don't.) Do you feel so fried and dazed you swear your skin is about to peel right off? Do you feel utterly besotted and utterly convinced you have no idea what you're doing? Then you're doing it right!"

There was a lot that I found frightening about becoming a mother, but what scared me most was to realize how dependent it would make me on other people. When I told my friend Victoria, who had two grown sons of her own, that I was pregnant, she told me to find women who have children and make friends, because I was going to need other moms.

By the time I brought home the baby, the order to make friends had fallen by the wayside. Everything went bananas the moment I went to the hospital to deliver. It took one emergency C-section, one three-unit blood transfusion, countless bags of IV blood pressure–lowering medication, and five days of recovery to understand that one does not assume the role of motherhood so much as explode into it.

Those first few weeks, scorched with fatigue, my ears rang and my eyes went hot and scratchy as though the insides of my lids had been sprinkled with sand. I swear I heard them scraping when I blinked. Terrorists use sleep deprivation as a form of torture, and now I knew why. Emotionally raw, physically sore, and a tired so far beyond tired, my first days at home with the baby were long and frantic. The nights, punctuated by the baby's colicky sleeplessness, felt psychedelic.

Every spiritual leader extols the divine purpose of motherhood, but then they tell you jack about how best to go about the day-to-day. They offer you no "keeping it real" counsel about the early days—that figuring out how the baby will sleep, and where and when and how and what the baby will eat, is trial and error.

If you want to force yourself to practice radical acceptance, start in the nursery. Accept that your new role is, among other things, being a human napkin. Surrender to the goop. Put burp clothes, rags, and wipes everywhere. On the back of every chair, over your shoulder, laced through the loop on your maternity jeans, which you are probably still wearing.

Accept that your brain is like polenta. When asked even the simplest questions, you will sound like a Mafia don in a legal deposition: *I do not know. I cannot remember. Not to my recollection. Not that I recall.* At some point, your brain will come back online. For the most part. I used to wonder why parents shared so many photos of their newborns on social media. Why so many pictures? I mean, you're right *there* with that kid, aren't you? When I became a mom I understood: It's not just because of the overwhelming love for your child, but also because on some level, you're aware that you're so fried, if you don't document those crazy, precious first weeks, you're liable to forget them. The baby book may stay blank, but the iPhone camera storage is maxed out.

And also, perhaps most important, accept that the title of World's Greatest Mother goes to no one. Feel free to let that aspiration go right away. The best, most amazing, affirming, life-giving, and life-saving advice came from my friend Alena, when I was newly pregnant and agonizing over what to do about work—should I take time off and suffer the financial hit, or should I scramble to find a decent sitter and re-enter the fray? As a corporate executive who has done everything from spend a week away from her kids on a business trip to renegotiating her contract to work at home, she said, "You're damned if you do, damned if you don't."

At first, her sentiment struck me as merciless, but it came to be invaluably soothing because it applied to every choice I confronted: working versus staying at home, breastfeeding versus bottle-feeding, sleep training in a crib or in a swing, cuddling or crying it out.

For every choice or sacrifice, there was an opposite choice or sacrifice that, once made, I'd probably doubt just as much. And I'd be judged either way. Parenting, I was coming to see, was like so much of adult existence—a series of best guesses. I looked forward to laughing about it, if I ever slept long enough to get my sense of humor back.

Raising a child is one big referendum on choices. Every trip out of the house with the baby became a slalom course of unsolicited advice. I learned this during a simple trip to the diner, with the baby tucked under her organic cotton Yankees blanket in the car carrier that Mike hoisted into the booth since I wasn't allowed to lift anything heavier than fifteen pounds.

Women, in particular, love to start up a chat. They like to ask about the baby's weight, whether or not she's sleeping through the night, whether or not you're breastfeeding. God, do they like to talk about breastfeeding. A pregnant woman is a public entity, so when you're pregnant, strangers try to pat your belly. But once the baby's born, they reach clear into your bra cups.

These conversations were hard for me, not just because of the invasive nature, but also because breastfeeding was, beyond the traumatic birth itself, where I most abruptly came up against the inadequacy of my body. I heard stories of so many new mothers who were wrung out with fatigue but untroubled by a baby who took to nursing "like a champ." Not me. I'd sweat to produce an ounce or two, which I'd administer to the baby in the tiny vial bottles meant for the colostrum you produce before your real milk came in. The baby slurped every drop in an instant, those few ounces the gateway drug, and I had nothing to offer as follow-up. When she was hungry again, she'd root, nudging her little face on my breast, turning her head from side to side to snuffle either cheek on my chest. The first of many ways I would come up short. If motherhood is anything, it's a crash course in finding your limitations.

The baby wouldn't latch, so I pumped. Pumping, when I handed the baby off to Mike, meant a half hour all to myself, uninterrupted. Stressful as pumping was, it became my downtime. I passed the minutes reading Anne Lamott's *Operating Instructions*, a journal of her son's first year, published in the 1990s and groundbreaking in its time for its unapologetic honesty. Anne is a fellow churchy type who likes to curse, so I thought that losing myself in her story would be the perfect pastime—her words an accompaniment to the pathetic *skreek skreek* of the manual breast pump, then, later, to the robotic *ka-chunka-chunk* of the electric Medela pump to which I upgraded in hopes of boosting my meager output.

But Lamott was one of those easy-feeding mamas, dedicating several passages to holy Madonna scenes of nursing, how it made her feel queenly and capable and incomparably bonded to her new son. I had assumed I'd be spending these elastic, crazy first days like her, with a sleepy, contented, milk-drunk baby draped on my shoulder. I'd probably have cracked and bloody nipples, but still. I felt so bad, so defective. What are our breasts meant to do if not this?

"Why don't you stick with formula?" Mike said. "It's good enough."

He didn't get it. Formula, every modern mother has been counseled, is shoddy goods. Breast is best. Or else.

I couldn't fail at this. I couldn't quit.

After trying every herb, poultice, supplement, and tonic, I drove with the baby to New Paltz to see Donna Bruschi, breastfeeding evangelist. Known for being able to conjure a good latch from even the most resistant infant and to urge dedication in the most frustrated mom, she spent ninety minutes observing me trying to feed the baby and giving us advice.

At the end, tucking her salt-and-pepper braid over her shoulder, she wrote some tips and read them aloud with the softest voice. "Just do what you can," she said. "Accept all efforts. If she gets 90 percent of her nutrition from formula, that's fine."

I couldn't believe what I was hearing and from whom I was hearing it. It was as though the pope were condoning my extramarital affair. But her permission to bottle-feed absolved me. For whatever reason, I needed another mother to let me off the hook. What I'd been waiting for all along was maternal dispensation.

I didn't feel sorry for myself, though my heart hurt for my baby. I realized that this was one of many limitations I'd have to woman up and face—that parenting is one giant ongoing lesson in adapting to things beyond your control. Of going with the flow. Or, in the case of my underperforming milk glands, the lack of it.

Beyond the breastfeeding struggle, what got to me most about the early days was the profound and immediate redistribution of time. Every second of my life was accounted for. I no longer slept in. I no longer followed my whim and stopped off for coffee, or went on a run simply because I felt like it. Hell, I no longer had ten minutes to stare into space.

The one thing I refused to lose among the demands of baby anarchy was a daily shower. Oh heck yes, I showered. I put the baby in the car seat right on the other side of the shower curtain and sang her favorite, "Row, Row, Row Your Boat," over the beating of the shower spray, as many times as I had to in order to keep her from crying until I was clean. I'd step out of the shower, wrap myself in a towel, and row the boat some more until I was dressed.

The days really were okay. The baby and I would sit outside, her little bassinet covered in mosquito mesh, and we'd take in the fresh summer air, her unfocused vision trained on the dancing green canopy of leaves overhead.

Nights, though, were hard. Somewhere in the midst of this shifting concept of time and how I'd be spending it, forever bound to this little, helpless person, I located a spiraling, celestial loneliness. A loneliness that felt very close to mourning—as if by becoming a mother, I'd lost an elemental part of myself. My old life hadn't been so bad, I realized. When the baby was particularly difficult, wriggling and wailing from reflux and general baby confusion, I feverishly missed how things had been. As much as I'd been in a hurry to get this motherhood thing started, I didn't for one second consider how much I'd grieve my autonomy, my ability to be indulgent with my time, with my things, with my shoes. I missed my old shoes, rendered unwearable by the spreading of my feet in the last months of pregnancy. I missed *me*. Grief, I began to see, is gratitude turned inside out. A rearview reappraisal of a good life now beyond my grasp.

As I sat with the baby in the dim nursery, feeding and rocking her, I kept thinking of the scene in *The Bell Jar* where Sylvia Plath's alter ego Esther Greenwood is watching from the sidelines at a party as two people fall in love with each other. "It's like watching Paris from an express caboose heading in the opposite direction—every second the city gets smaller and smaller, only you feel it's really you getting smaller and smaller and lonelier and lonelier, rushing away from all those lights and excitement at about a million miles an hour."[1]

I felt, in that quiet, safe room, that even though I had supposedly assumed my biggest and most serious role of my life, I was getting smaller and more insignificant. Not even on a train, but on a raft drifting farther out, the sight of the shoreline falling away. This was all I'd wanted for so long. I now could claim residency on the island, a native. I couldn't be voted off, or exiled from the tribe. So why this? Why now?

I prayed to the heavens for the ability to reconcile this rift in my heart. *God, I need you now. Help me heal this because I sure can't turn back. Oh, and while you're at it, can you get this poor baby of mine a good four-hour stretch of sleep? We'd both appreciate it.*

Everyone tells you to sleep when the baby sleeps, but the baby would only sleep in twenty-minute bursts, and I was hungry for connection, so when she slept, I went online. Like a Richard Scarry storybook, the busy village in the computer had a million bustling, engaging activities to track.

Facebook and Twitter became a techno-umbilicus to the outside world, a way to assure myself that the old life—albeit a virtual one—was still there. My friends were still there, the news rolled on, new memes and cat photos popped up to amuse me. When my husband went back to work, the phone became Mommy's little helper. I felt less alone with it by my side. As much as people asserted that I should *definitely call if I needed anything* and they would *totally come over, I mean it!* the problem was I usually needed them between four and seven in the morning.

Who's there for you at that time? You know who: Facebook.

Clicking through a parenting site, I saw a comic panel of a mother breastfeeding her child on a bed, her face twisted in panic as she cast about with her foot to try to capture a cell phone that had slipped from her grasp while the baby suckled. Was this motherhood now—no longer a real-life community but a range of lonely eyes scanning in the darkness, our faces lit by phone screens? If it takes a village, maybe we're finding it online.

I tried to stay on top of the headlines, but I couldn't read news stories about bad things that involved children. If I was a lightweight about these things before, I was positively helpless against the horror now. An illness, an accident, abuse—the depth and breadth of suffering that befell innocent children made me shut my eyes and ball my fists at my temples. What shocked me was how utterly physical my fear and revulsion were—my stomach so tight I almost doubled over at the pain of it. The dread haunted me.

The baby's naptime became "Scary Mommy" time, when I'd read the mothering website's anonymous confessions section, which provided a font of assurance that I wasn't the only one who feared that underneath it all, I was screwing up this motherhood thing royally.

I read about mothers who want to run away. About mothers who run up secret debt. Mothers who can't get through the day without a drink or a joint. *This* was the mothering manual everyone needed— not how to do it, but how it's really done, imperfectly, with a lot of fear and self-doubt. I don't think I could've been a mother one moment sooner than now, the age of TMI, because all of this faceless, raw, maternal oversharing saved my sanity. Discretion is no friend to the new mother, and the Internet is a small white room, every surface padded, where we can yell and cry and kick it all out—ragtag testimony meets cyber-confessional. All these women howling into a great, yawning chasm, knowing that their words, their frustrations, their heartaches, are reaching a sympathetic audience. Can I get a witness?

Yes. Scream it out, sister.

God answered my prayers not by removing the conflict in my heart, but by leading me to a place where I could see how common that conflict really was. All mothers were on the verge of tearing out our hair. We all felt broken and desperate and exhausted, and we all were madly in love beyond any comprehension. Online I felt so much less alone, and that was what I needed most. Again, I was reminded: never underestimate the healing power of "Me too."

The Internet bought me some free time, too, in the form of cloyingly sweet songs from Little Baby Bum videos on YouTube. "The Wheels on the Bus" sung in Alvin-and-the-Chipmunks-like voices may make you want to stab yourself in the neck with a sippy cup straw, but it gave you time to elbow a frozen lasagna into the oven or fold some towels. At some point I noted that the most popular Little Baby Bum video had been played almost a billion times inside of a year, that number representing countless parents trying to distract the kid long enough to run to the bathroom or bag up the trash. The Internet hit-counter as truth-teller, the oracle of our age.

Still, for all the challenges that came with my baby, I liked her so much. I'd marvel as I rocked her, standing at the front window as evening consumed the day, both of us watching the darkening world outside, a bond of just us two: *You like looking at the moon? I also like looking at the moon!* During the day, she'd hang out in her little sit-me-up seat and stare into my face while I sang to her. "Row, row, row your boat . . ." She'd grin and grin, like, "This is the best story I have ever heard!" *Moby-Dick* for the footie-pajamas set.

Yes, I was exhausted. Yes, I was lonely. But I was a mother. For every sacrifice that would be asked of me, for every ounce of physical endurance I was called to give beyond my limits, it hurt less than the ache of empty arms. I was too frantic to spend much time in prayer, so instead, as I sat with her, I said, "Thank you for this child, God. Thank you for this child. I don't know what to ask you for, so send me whatever you know I need."

One afternoon as the baby napped facedown against my shoulder and I stared at my phone screen around her rising and falling back, a Facebook message pinged my phone. It was my new mom-friend Sarah, who lived forty minutes north in the Hudson Valley woods. Unlike me, Sarah was a lactating overachiever.

"Listen, I have over a gallon of breast milk stored . . ." she wrote with a little baby bottle emoji.

How nice for you, I thought glumly.

Another message from Sarah: "Do you want it?"

Breast milk is called *liquid gold* for a reason—when sold through a third-party medical supplier, it costs four dollars an ounce or more. The phrase "no use crying over spilled milk" must have referenced a woman like me who spent two hours pumping for a single crummy ounce. What Sarah was offering me was worth a small fortune monetarily, and worth even more emotionally. I pictured the baby sitting in a corner, a plastic gallon jug upended as she guzzled down Sarah's whole batch of vegan premium, pumped with loving ease. I had tasted my breast milk once out of curiosity—it was sweet, like melted vanilla ice cream. Small wonder the kid was hooked. Grateful tears dripped on my phone screen as I tapped back a thank you, and that I'd think about it.

And I did think about it. I thought hard about how much the nutrients would benefit my baby. But I also pictured tiny premature babies in incubators and babies with immune problems and babies who, despite every effort, failed to thrive, all of whom would need the breast milk so much more than my daughter, who was plumping up nicely, alert and hardy. I messaged Sarah that I was deeply grateful, but that the best thing she could do to help me was to donate the milk to a NICU, where it was urgently needed.

For days afterward, I couldn't think about Sarah's offer without crying, and there was something baptismal about those tears, as if by running down my face, they'd ritualistically ushered me into someplace new, someplace more raw and deeply feeling. If despair slices through you more physically when you become a mother, so, too, does kindness.

Within two months of giving birth, my blood pressure was lower, I had lost over thirty pounds of water weight, and I had accepted that "anarchy on a plate" was going to be the theme of my life for a while. Now medically cleared to hoist the baby in her carrier, I was ready for a night out, to introduce the baby to my book group. Sporting a ponytail, tinted lip balm, and tinted sunscreen, I felt like I was headed to the Met Gala. I packed her diaper bag and drove across the Hudson as the late-afternoon sun tilted against the horizon, the river a flat ribbon sparkling around the hills. I pulled onto the host's quiet tree-lined street, picked up the car carrier, and walked the baby down the block, riding a gust of survivor's euphoria.

Everyone in Jill's small living room angled to hold the baby, each well practiced in how to talk to a new mom, saying these three lines with utmost sincerity: "You're doing awesome!" "You look great!" "Your baby is so adorable!"

After being cooed at and cradled in six pairs of strangers' arms, the baby started fussing. Determined to be the mom who spared people the agita of infant tantrums, I grabbed her bottle and stepped out onto Jill's porch while everyone helped herself to fancy sandwiches from the local deli.

The baby and I, the pack of two, paced the porch, the old, grey-stained floorboards creaking. I pointed out the local plants to her—day lilies, black-eyed Susans, hydrangea bushes, their pompom flowers pink from the alkaline soil.

The screen door slammed. Erin, who had five-year-old twins and a seven-year-old back at home, and Maura, whose daughter was in her thirties, had come outside so I didn't have to stand on the porch alone with my squalling baby.

On a paper plate, Erin had a roasted eggplant, tomato, and mozzarella sandwich on an olive oil–brushed baguette. The smell of the rosemary from the bread was divine. "Are you hungry?"

I tried to shift the baby into one arm, but she started screaming. "I don't have a free hand."

Erin took the sandwich from the paper plate and held it up so I could take some bites as the baby drank from her bottle, while Maura told me about how she didn't breastfeed her daughter even once when she was an infant. Maura was single at the time, with a full-time job outside the home, and she simply hadn't the time or the ability to feed her any other way.

The scent of honeysuckle wrapped around the three of us, the breeze blowing the aroma from the verdant tangle of vines that climbed the wooden fence running the length of the driveway. And that was my dinner—parenting shoptalk and a sandwich held up to my mouth by another mom so I could eat it, bite by clumsy bite, tearing through the thick, oily bread with my front teeth. What I had been told at the beginning was true—you really do need other moms, and they need you just as much. Me for you, you for me, in ways both large and small.

In person or even online, through the presence and reassurance of other mothers, the intolerable becomes bearable and the impossible becomes doable, reminding us that no matter how lonely we feel, no mom is an island. Motherhood can be hard, frightening, and isolating. Yet somehow we find each other. We click and blink in the dark, buoy lights bobbing in unfamiliar water, locating and saving each other every day. It takes so little to make us feel so alone, but then, it also takes so little to remind us that we're in the same boat, natives at sea off the Isle of Mom, storm-tossed, crazy, ecstatic, and rowing safe to shore.

13

THIS IS MY BLOOD

In my infant daughter's palm, the gold crucifix looked as if it were resting on the belly of a chubby pink starfish. Its fine chain wound once around her wrist, trailing across a white baptism shawl trimmed in fringe. The necklace was a family heirloom handed down from the baby's namesake—her long-departed paternal great-grandmother. Before we left for the church, the godmother, my sister-in-law Lisa, had draped the chain around the baby's neck and closed the clasp.

Much has been made of the Francis Effect—the magnetic, humanitarian charm of His Holiness, Pope Francis—drawing back parishioners who had given up on the church, but it also extends to those of us who might have never been drawn to Catholicism in the first place. When the Francis Effect landed at our doorstep, it inspired me to entrust the Catholic Church with no less than my daughter's spiritual heart.

When my husband and I, ten years into our marriage, discussed having a child, there was much to consider. Could we afford it? Did we have the energy? Then, a question that took me quite by surprise: Would you, Mike asked, be willing to raise the baby Catholic?

My introduction to Catholicism was inauspicious. In 2003, my husband and I, still newlyweds, arrived at West Point. At the newcomers' fair, we stopped to chat with the priest from the post's Catholic chapel. Mike explained that we'd had a hasty legal marriage before he deployed, but we were interested in a church ceremony.

"It might be a little complicated," my husband said. "You see, I'm divorced . . ." The priest winced. "And the marriage wasn't annulled." A prickling, uneasy heat traveled up my legs. "And my wife isn't Catholic." The priest winced again.

We waited for the priest to say something about helping us plan, or at least invite us to his parish office for further discussion.

"Mike, to be honest," the priest said, "I'm worried about your mortal soul."

My husband looked like he'd been gut-shot.

I was speechless. Who says that? Who *thinks* that?

Over a decade later, I agreed, after much deliberation, to a Catholic upbringing for our daughter. Why? The cheeky answer would be that marriage involves compromise, even if I make it only a biannual event. In seriousness, credit is due, in no small part, to His Holiness. In his view, our interfaith union is a blessing, not an abomination. He has said that any Christian marriage is a "real vocation, just like priesthood and religious life."[1] If he held a scorched-earth view like that Army priest, I wouldn't have considered it, but Francis carries the marks of a social reformer, on this issue and several others. Where

I once saw intimidation, I now saw promise. That the pontiff once worked as a bouncer only added to his credibility.

I worried that antireligion or atheist friends would assume that willingness to have my daughter baptized represented a drift toward the fanatical on my part. But baptism, I found, can bring out a softness even in the most cynical. Maybe because there is a child involved. Maybe there's something about innocence that reaches us where intellect cannot.

A baptism can turn into a ritual done by rote, the purpose obscured by the busywork of shopping for the white dress, ordering invitations, planning the lunch. Hostess anxiety kicked in. Did I want to serve chicken Marsala or orecchiette with broccoli rabe and sausage?

The wrong dress was delivered, a stiff organza festooned with iridescent sequins that resembled an elaborate lampshade. The bakery promised a cake with a cross of pink frosting roses—I pictured the blush of a new petal or ballet slippers. Instead, I opened the box to find a shade that could best be described as Vegas Bordello, or possibly Flamingo Explosion.

Intention returned to the fore when we sat down with Sister Kathy for the pre-baptism interview at the local parish. Gentle and kind, she saw no issue with ours being an interfaith marriage, and the fate of our mortal souls was not brought into question. At the conclusion, she asked, "What do you like about the Catholic Church, and what would you like to see change?"

My husband felt that priests should be allowed to marry and have families, and that divorced parishioners and non-Catholics should be permitted to take communion. I wanted to see women in governing roles, as well as significant advancement on gay and transgender issues. I had so many "recovering Catholic" friends who were deeply church-bruised, vowing never to return. Would being raised in

Catholicism make my daughter feel ashamed of her body, like my friend Susie's mother, who went to a convent school where the nuns shook talcum powder into the bathwater so you couldn't see yourself and get any sinful ideas? Would she feel broken, judged, or scorned were she to divorce, like my husband, or never to marry at all? Would she feel diminished, knowing that no matter how devoted she might be, the role of church leadership was a door closed to her? With so many doubts and anxieties, agreeing to this felt as superstitious as rolling dice to determine a solution to a problem.

What about Catholicism appealed to me? Despite not feeling the call to conversion, there was much that I loved. The prominence of Mary and the saints, and the sensory richness of Mass—the colors and the Latin recitations, the heady incense as the censer swings by. I even enjoyed getting in the communion line to receive a blessing, crossing my arms over my chest to indicate my non-Catholic status and doing a polite bowing curtsy, similar to a cotillion dip, as the priest blessed me. I admired the stark, bloody sincerity of the crucified Jesus on the cross over the altar, so raw in comparison to the tidy, bare, post-resurrection cross that hangs in a Presbyterian church. I respected the rituals woven into everyday life of the culturally Catholic: crossing yourself in a moment of duress or gratitude, or appealing to Saint Anthony when you've misplaced something. *Saint Anthony, Saint Anthony, please come down. What was lost must now be found*—a ritual as faithfully followed as Italians tossing coins into the backseat of a new car for good luck.

When I was first trying to get pregnant, a procession honoring the Feast of Saint Anthony came rolling down Lisa's street in Brooklyn while we were visiting. A small brass band played, the statue of Saint Anthony moving slowly along Cropsey Avenue as it was pulled by devotees from the local parish, pots of white stargazer lilies encircling his feet. Chains of dollar bills attached to white, red, and green ribbons fluttered against his robes. Mike pressed money into my palm, and for my offering, I was given a laminated prayer card with an embedded pewter Saint Anthony medal and a flour-dusted Italian bun. I looked up Saint Anthony when I got home that night, and found that he's not only the patron saint of lost objects but also of fertility and pregnant women. I wrapped the bread in tinfoil and placed it in the freezer for safekeeping. Bread in the freezer, bun in the oven. The coincidence of the procession with our visit to a house on the traditional route felt portentous. Maybe Saint Anthony knew something I didn't.

Around the robust Christian comedy circuit, Presbyterians are referred to as "the Frozen Chosen." Certainly our buttoned-up austerity has its limits. Despite the reservations I had about Catholicism, I love that there's something so upfront about it, as though you can reach right in and feel its pulse, alive and leaping.

The interview with Sister Kathy illuminated where my husband and I were yoked together, our respect for tradition entwined with the possibility of progress. Our emotional stake in the sacrament became heart-piercingly clear: when you baptize a child, you're voting for hope.

The weekend before the baptism, my friend Linda Jiménez was ordained at the storied Fifth Avenue Presbyterian Church in Manhattan. A swarm of clergy stood for her, at least thirty of them female. Down in the front pews, I saw our friend John Russell Stanger, the first out LGBTQ Presbyterian minister ordained in Texas, in his white alb and nose ring.

Linda brought her own style to the ceremony, in a nod to her Pentecostal roots. She took up a microphone and delivered a blistering gospel solo rendition of "We Come This Far by Faith," after which a man behind me sniffed, "Well, she's got some Pentecostal tendencies, but I think she'll do all right," which may be the whitest compliment ever given. After a dozen or so delighted clergy people surrounded Linda for a laying on of hands, she delivered her first communion as pastor.

Reverend Anita, who had just presented Linda with her minister's robe and stole, held the tray of bread. As I tore off a piece, she said, "This is my body."

Praise be to God.

I dipped my bread in the chalice Linda held. "This is my blood."

Praise be to God.

I returned to my seat, happy to have received not only the blessing of communion but the privilege of witnessing a young woman poised to embark on a powerful journey. How wonderful to have so many years of evolution ahead of her. Years of being part of the solution. What a gift.

On the day of the baptism, Lisa dressed the baby in a simple white cotton gown bordered in thick, old-fashioned daisy lace. She fastened the pearl buttons up the back, one, two, three, and tied the long sash into a bow.

The slant of the afternoon sun through the stained glass cast jewel-toned panels of light on the sanctuary floor. The priest dipped his fingers in chrism, touched the top of my daughter's head, then reached under her collar and dabbed the oil on a spot over her little hummingbird heart.

At the altar, my husband tilted our drowsy daughter over the marble basin, and the priest took up the silver baptismal shell, the holy water running in rivulets through her dark hair. In the name of the Father, the Son, and the Holy Spirit, love built a bridge between two denominations and two families, reaching across the aisle and out into the world, anointed.

Nailed to the doorframe, next to a stand of red votive candles in the vestibule, was a small stoup of holy water. I saw my stepson Chris dip his fingers in and cross himself as he left the church, giving me a sweet stab of tenderness. Proclaimed atheist or not, his reflexes were still Catholic. Maybe he'd circle back to this church as his baby sister grew into it. Yes, I wanted her to be the same religion as her big brothers. The boys had given her such an openhearted welcome, Chris bringing a baby gift from their mother of nursery rhyme books, an outfit with kitten faces on it, and a hippo rattle, and Mike sitting in the living room armchair with her, giving her bottle after bottle. God might bring our family from blended to fused in spirit.

As we drove from the church, we passed a statue of Christ, his arms extended. We had passed the rite of baptism down to yet another generation—how far back had it gone on either side of our families? Decades? Centuries? My daughter was now included in that chain of life. I looked at her reflection in the mirror above her car seat and prayed: *I give her to you, God. She's both yours and ours, yet at the same time, she belongs to no one but herself.*

At the restaurant, we swapped the baby's christening gown for pink cotton footie pajamas with owls on the front, and I folded the dress carefully, to be delivered to the cleaners for archival storage. Might our baby girl have a daughter of her own whom she'd baptize in the same dress? It was hard to have such a grown-up thought for a tiny person who had only recently figured out how to hold up her own head.

After lunch, coffee and dessert were passed around. While my daughter lounged in her father's lap, I tapped the side of my water goblet with the blade of my knife. Everyone raised a glass. What to say?

I remembered departed family with us in spirit. I thought of Linda, coming into her own as a minister. I wondered about this faith into which my daughter had been welcomed, no way of knowing that weeks later, the pope would demote prominent cardinal Raymond Burke, who has criticized the pontiff's relatively progressive tone on issues such as homosexuality and abortion. Then, weeks later, Sister Donna Markham, a Dominican nun, was named the first female leader of Catholic Charities USA, thus affirming that the church, like a child, can grow right before your eyes.

Parental patience, however, is still required, given the pope's comments during a Mass held in Manila, that "the family is threatened by growing efforts on the part of some to redefine the very institution of marriage . . . These realities are increasingly under attack from powerful forces, which threaten to disfigure God's plan for creation,"[2] which many are interpreting as a hardline stance against gay marriage. Yikes.

Back to the toast. I took a breath and kept it simple. "God bless the friends and relatives who make up our family. Let's have some cake."

14

⁂

LETTER TO MY
(POSSIBLE) SON

My darling daughter:
  I've been meaning to write you this letter in case you need it when you're older, but I thought I could put it off for at least a couple of years. Now, after hearing about the suicide of Leelah Alcorn, I feel an urgency to get this down.

Leelah, feeling socially isolated and rejected by her Christian parents, stepped in front of a passing semitrailer on southbound Interstate 71 in Union Township, Ohio, on a quiet Sunday morning. She was just seventeen. She was transgender.

Right now, you're not even a year old, far too young to understand.

As a mother, her death breaks my heart. As a Christian, it moves me to speak.

When I was a few months pregnant with you and learned that you were a girl, I was thrilled. Despite the bandied-about opinion that girls are so much harder and that girls are such trouble, I couldn't wait to tell everyone: *Team Pink!*

On the sunny spring afternoon that you were born, the nurses wrapped you in a blanket and put a tiny, gender-neutral pink-and-blue-striped cap on your little head. They brought you over to me, and as soon as I started speaking to you, my voice a steady coo, you settled, and I knew that you were my daughter.

But what if it turns out you aren't?

What if you are actually my son?

The year of your birth, 2014, presented a giant leap for transgender visibility. The suicide of dear Leelah, however, tells us that we still have so very far to go.

Say that as the years go by, and as your body, mind, and identity mature, you find that your physical self doesn't match your sense of your own gender. What if, female body aside, you believe you're male? What if you feel no gender at all? How will I raise you? How will I love you?

The same. I will raise you and love you just the same.

When Leelah came out as transgender to her parents, her mother, an avowed Christian, told Leelah that her gender identity was a phase, that she would never truly be a girl, and that God doesn't make mistakes. They prohibited her from social media and subjected her to a retinue of Christian therapists. They told her she was selfish and wrong and that she should look to God for help.

I don't think God makes mistakes either. The first commandment of child-rearing is to parent the child you have, not the child you wish you had. I can think of no greater emotional sin than rejecting a kid for who they really are.

Trans children deserve to be treated like divine beings, not pathologies. They are to be nurtured and supported, not cured. Conversion therapy has a disastrous success rate; and isolation, it has been proven over and over again, is deadly, a fact made obvious by Leelah's suicide.

Make no mistake, my daughter, we are raising you in a Christian home—albeit a multidenominational one. A Presbyterian Celtic cross hangs in the front hallway, and the gold heirloom crucifix you wore at your Catholic baptism rests in a music box on your dresser. Should your path be similar to Leelah's, I want you to know that, yes, you *can* look to God for help. Not for help in overcoming your transgenderism, but rather in finding a bulwark against the prejudice you encounter in the face of it.

Being honest about who you are may make some people uncomfortable, but it will also make you many true and devoted friends. I have learned this lesson several times over. I will introduce you to Reverend Allyson Robinson, a trans Baptist minister and West Point graduate who focused on social justice while at seminary. I will introduce you to Reverend Lia Scholl, an ally in the South who has centered ministering to the marginalized since she was ordained. Your auntie Kate Bornstein, one of the great transgender spirits of our time, is ready to sit down and talk about God—and whether you think God is really a he. (I, personally, think God is neither a he nor a she but a "Whoa!") These friends of mine will be yours too. I saw it on the day of your baptism: God's love shines through stained glass in a rainbow. Embrace everybody.

A few years back, Nichole Nordeman's song "Brave" was a huge hit on Christian radio. The lyrics describe a woman saying good-bye to the status quo because God had made her brave enough to follow her own road. To be true to herself.

These lyrics describe exactly how I'd like you to relate to God—as a support for becoming who you really are meant to be, and as a safe spot on a risky journey. Should your road to authentic gender identity be rocky, may you see God as an ally, not an adversary: a force that makes you want to be brave.

Please know there are many churches, organizations, and clergy who will welcome you, unreservedly. I hope that as time passes, acceptance becomes the dominant image of the American Christian, instead of the stiff, blinkered, fear-driven Jesus Machine that seems to be holding sway today. Like many other believers, I am so very, very tired of intolerance and willful ignorance dressed in the guise of Christian principles. I almost swore off the church for good because of this.

Please know, also, that you would not be the first transgender member of this family. Grandma (my mother) told us when we were kids about her cousin John becoming Jenny, way back in the 1970s, when transgenderism was much less understood or tolerated than it is today. Do you know how your grandma reacted? She smiled at the idea, then got on with her life, and never said one bad thing about her cousin. As for Jenny, when she transitioned, she was already in her thirties and married with children. She kept on with her successful law practice, and, over the years, welcomed a pack of grandchildren, who love her and are made better by her loving presence in return.

If you're wondering how I had time to produce this letter with you in my care: I frantically wrote while your aunt, the Presbyterian minister, babysat. After entertaining you with an iPhone playlist of children's playroom classics like "The Farmer in the Dell," peppy Christian day camp songs, and Jimmy Buffet, she read to you from a gift she brought, *Baby's First Photo Bible.* Quote therein: Jesus loves *all* the little children of the world.

You will always be my child, but your gender identity will always be your own. If you grow into a strapping young man, your Army dad will teach you how to put a proper shine on a black leather boot. If you end up a high-flying femme, I will blow glitter on your wings. If on your wedding day, I end up straightening your tie instead of smoothing your veil, I will do it with greatest pride and, I'm sure, more than a few shameless tears. (Be warned, though: whether you mature into a heterosexual girly-girl, a bisexual butch, or a queer transman, you can count on me *skootching* for a grandbaby or two. Sorry, kid. Nobody's perfect!)

Jack Kerouac said, "Nothing else in the world matters but the kindness of Grace, God's gift to suffering mortals."[1] In the horrific loss of Leelah Alcorn, grace appears as the opportunity to agitate for change: to educate and to affirm the core goodness of Christianity. At the end of her suicide note, she wrote,

> The only way I will rest in peace is if one day transgender people aren't treated the way I was, when they're treated like humans, with valid feelings and human rights. Gender needs to be taught about in schools, the earlier the better. My death needs to mean something. My death needs to be counted in the number of transgender people who commit suicide this year. I want someone to look at that number and say "that's [messed] up" and fix it. Fix society. Please.[2]

As a mother, as an activist, as a Christian, I will do my best. And I am not alone.

My beautiful child, may you always know love for who you are. If you can't count on that from the world, know that you can at least count on that from me. For Leelah, for every transgender, genderfluid, or gender-transcending soul, I make this pledge: I may not succeed in fixing society, but I will never stop trying. God as my witness.

Love forever,

Mom[3]

15

CATHOLIC GIRLS
DO IT BETTER

When a scab on my friend Mary Beth's scalp wouldn't heal, she made an appointment with a dermatologist. After a ten-minute examination, followed by a hasty referral to an oncologist, my friend—my witty, sentimental, kick-ass mom friend—went from being a "lady with a skin thing" to a woman with a diagnosis of advanced malignant melanoma.

Mary Beth had the cancerous lesion removed. But within months, the cancer came back, metastasized to her lungs and soft tissue, and was classified as stage four. To clarify her diagnosis, Mary Beth said, "If you want to know how bad this is, there is no stage five."

Even as Mary Beth's illness was unfolding, I had trouble believing it was real. Here was this woman, the most alert and juicy woman I knew, having to contend with the grim news that she might die. The very notion seemed impossible. Mary Beth, a Jersey girl like me, had a singular knack for seeking out the affordable pleasures of New York City: finding the perfect Vivienne Tam sheath dress on the clearance rack at TJ Maxx; standing in line for hours for Shakespeare in the Park; scheduling her day so she could drop in to City Bakery for the hot chocolate topped with a homemade marshmallow, a dense white square big enough to stopper the paper cup it's served in.

Mary Beth had an eye for refined beauty too. On a trip to Kleinfeld in Brooklyn to help our friend choose her wedding gown, Mary Beth made a surgical strike in the couture section. The bride's mother had built a small-business empire, and her only child's wedding was a "sky's the limit" affair. As we walked toward the private fitting suite, passing thousands of gowns, Mary Beth reached into a packed-full rack and grabbed an ivory Duchesse satin Reem Acra, strapless with a full skirt and a wide Wedgewood blue satin hip sash, and no other dress came close. Standing on her circular platform in the fitting suite to model the dress, our friend looked like a John Singer Sargent model with a pixie cut. High culture or lowbrow, Mary Beth had a gift for delight.

Shortly after her diagnosis and first surgery, during one of our walk-and-talks through the Museum of Modern Art, things took an unexpected turn near the Chagall: Mary Beth started talking about God. Our beliefs, which we'd kept out of view of each other since we'd met fifteen years earlier working at the same magazine in San Francisco, were having a meet-cute moment.

"How did I not know this about you?" she said.

"How did *I* not know this about *you*?"

"I've always been this way. Jesus is my man."

We pushed through the museum's tall glass doors and kept our conversation going down 54th Street. We veered off the sidewalk and into a shopping mews across the street from the Ziegfeld Theater. We huddled on a concrete step, pouring out our shy, churchy hearts. She said she took her daughters Lucy and Bea to mass every Sunday; I said I'd gathered enough evidence to believe that God exists but that I felt bad that I needed the evidence at all. She told me she understood. Still feeling anxious about this church thing, I felt weird talking about it—I've heard friends confess to crimes with less trepidation.

I was so relieved to find out that a friend believed as I did. Our friendship grew a new dimension—one of the best things that can happen, ever, like the come-true version of the city-dwellers' dream in which they discover their apartment has an extra room they'd never known about. Our relationship, which had spanned several moves around the country and several years, was strange and beautiful, and now our shared love of God was strange and beautiful too.

Mary Beth prayed for a miracle, and science answered the call. Through the referral of a friend, she applied and gained entry into a clinical trial to test a form of immunotherapy that prompted the body's own defenses to attack and obliterate cancer cells. The treatment was grueling and required frequent trips to Sloan Kettering to have the drug combination administered under tightly controlled conditions. She had to endure constant blood draws, sometimes giving as many as thirty tubes in a single visit.

When she started treatment, I gave her a small, translucent, red glass heart I'd bought as a souvenir on a trip to Europe, a good luck charm as close as I could get to an ex-voto. I'm not above the superstitious rituals I developed in my witchy Goth phase. I would pray for her, but I wanted to cover all the bases.

We arranged to meet on the steps of the Metropolitan Museum, one of our favorite places to spend a few precious hours together, after she was at the hospital for lab work and scans. She climbed out of the cab looking pale and tired, but she smiled.

When she hugged me, I could feel her ribs through her thin T-shirt. "I haven't eaten," she said. "I have to have an empty stomach for the lab results to be accurate."

There was a food truck parked at the curb selling the range of New York snacks—Snapple, coffee, hot dogs, knishes, chips, pretzels, and ice cream. "Dude, do you need a pretzel?"

"Yes," she said. "An emergency pretzel." We walked to the truck, arms linked. She pumped a figure eight of mustard onto the pretzel, then tore off a doughy, salty nub and gave it to me.

Inside the museum, we made our way through the sculptures in the Greek and Roman galleries, admiring the exquisite marble forms. Art is God's way of helping us humans wrap our puny brains around the existence of the divine, as there is no logical explanation for either talent, inspiration, or the pleasure they both can bring. Sneaky trick, and I dig it.

Mary Beth motioned me down a hallway. "This way. I want to show you the tooth."

I didn't know what she meant. Tooth? What tooth? An Andy Warhol tooth in the modern art wing? I followed her through a Renaissance portrait hall and into a gallery of religious artifacts— jeweled censers and gold busts of saints and miniature pietàs carved from ivory. We stopped in front of an illuminated case. Inside rested an ornate reliquary housing what was believed to be Mary Magdalene's tooth.

Only someone who knew me as well as Mary Beth would get how much I'd enjoy seeing Mary Magdalene's tooth, encased in an outsize crystal egg suspended by spires of gilded copper. Mary Beth loved rococo religiosity even more than I did: she brought back an entire suitcase full of Infant of Prague figurines when she went to the Czech Republic. We could make an entire, blissful day out of marveling at the artistic flourishes of suffering and penitence at The Cloisters— the demons painstakingly carved into the marble column tops! The sorrow in Mary's face in the seventeenth-century wood pietà! In art, the passion of Christianity is palpable. And where expressions of devotion are concerned, the Catholics are Marlon Brando yelling, *"Stella!"* in *A Streetcar Named Desire*.

At a lecture I attended called "Walking with God Through Pain and Suffering," pastor Timothy Keller of New York's Redeemer Presbyterian Church advised those interacting with someone in crisis—that is to say, all of us at some point—to refrain from saying, "It was God's plan." It can be seen as insensitive—"tough luck" dressed up in a Sunday bonnet. A *minister* telling people not to say "It was God's plan"—I was surprised, and relieved. I've always bridled against the sentiment, as if *that's* supposed to make someone feel better. He also counseled against saying, "God never gives us more than we can handle," "That which doesn't kill us makes us stronger," and "Everything happens for a reason."

I'd always hated these responses myself. They seem so tone-deaf and blamey, as if accepting God's plan were supposed to be effortless when it fact it's one of the most difficult things we are challenged to do. Pain can't be waved away with a platitude.

Reverend Keller also said, "Of all the religions in the world,

Christianity alone offers someone like Jesus, who not only suffers for you, but he suffers with you." I knew I could speak these words right into Mary Beth's heart—and for that I loved her. We could take comfort from this together, even if it was wildly Jesus-y, to the point of seeming kind of nuts. Yes, we have an invisible friend, and yes, he steeps in empathy so profound he bears its scars in his own skin. You don't lay that concept on just anyone. But I believed it, and so did she, and we passed it back and forth between us like a torch. Hope relayed.

I understood by now that God *did* have a plan for Mary Beth, but I also understood that it would be unknowable, and if I did find out what it was, unfortunately, I may not like it. To frame this in theological terms: cancer sucks.

Cancer is one of those experiences so far beyond anything I'd endured that there was no way I could say to Mary Beth that I understood what she was going through. I couldn't relate; I could only listen. To let what was sorrowful be sorrowful; to let what was awful stand revealed in its awfulness. Let be. Let be. Maybe that's a good default strategy for a friend in crisis: If you can't do "Me too," then how about "I'm here"?

"I could be fatalistic about my chances, or I could be optimistic," Mary Beth said over lunch at Le Pain Quotidien when she was halfway through the first phase of the clinical trial. I was having a salad, pretending to be virtuous, she a tartine and cake, with no interest in the charade. "Honestly," she said, "optimism is much harder."

Now that I was feeling better, I wanted to do better. But I had Pollyanna paralysis—there was so much wrong with the world, I didn't know where to start to fix it. Mary Beth was terribly ill. More than anything else, I wanted to fix my friend, but I couldn't.

We sometimes feel that what we do can't possibly be enough, so we stay frozen in place, doing nothing. How do we unthaw, reversing that paralysis? How do we choose our "cause"? We can go with what brings us to our knees, following the pain like a trail of guiding stars. We can also go to places we can reasonably reach. Sometimes we're so burdened ourselves, the most we can do is hold open doors for others and smile at strangers.

I wanted to forward Mary Beth articles on healing through diet, suggest acupuncturists, implore her to tell me about how she was feeling—"No, really. How *are* you?" But I kept myself in check, for her sake. Restraint can be its own form of care.

Poet Chris Abani said, "What I've come to learn is that the world is never saved in grand messianic gestures, but in the simple accumulation of gentle, soft, almost invisible acts of compassion."[1]

Inspiration struck. I knew what I would do for Mary Beth—I'd make her a dinner, something uncomplicated, a couple of potpies.

I set the oven to 350 degrees and pushed up my sleeves. I rolled out the piecrust dough so it lined the inside of the pans, scooped in the mixture of chicken chunks, peas, diced carrots, chopped onions, and corn in thick gravy, then covered it all with a sheet of dough that I crimped around the edges and baked them until they were golden brown and bubbling at the edges. I pulled them from the oven, the smell of hot, chickeny gravy rising from the crescent slits in the crust. Two perfect specimens—pretty as the Wakefield twins from Sweet Valley High. Mike and I drove to Inwood to drop the pies off, Mary Beth, Bea, and Lucy meeting us on the sidewalk, our offering received with smiles.

How much later did I learn that Mary Beth and her family were totally maxed out on potpies? Seems that everyone's potpie-baking impulse was activated by her dire situation, and she was inundated. I imagined the four of them trying to consume dozens of potpies, like Lucy and Ethel shoving chocolates into their mouths as the bonbons tumbled down the conveyer belt in the candy factory.

Cooking is a tangible way to show love, but asking the sick person if they'd like you to cook for them, and what they want to have, if so, is a way to refine it. A freezer can hold only so many good intentions.

In the midst of Mary Beth's drug trial, when everything tasted funny and her appetite was poor, she wanted a trip to Coney Island for a hot dog and a side of fries at Nathan's.

The November day was foggy and windy, the low cloud cover over Coney Island making a dome that amplified the screech of the subway cars as they rounded the curve into the Stillwell Avenue terminal. Mary Beth met me under the neon sign of a blinking hot dog wearing a bowtie and chef's toque. The amusement park rides were shut down, and Astroland was all but abandoned, but Nathan's was packed. We took our green plastic tray loaded with hot dogs, cheese fries, and Cokes to a high-topped table and ate standing up.

After lunch, we walked down the windy boardwalk to the aquarium and watched the walrus show, their big rubbery bodies flopping up and out of the pool at the command of their wet-suited trainers, and stopped by the penguin exhibit, the rocks of their enclosure streaked with white droppings. ("Crap happens," say both the Buddhists and Mother Nature.) We talked and walked among glowing tanks of silvery manta rays flapping slowly back and forth as if pacing to pass the time, and coral-studded reefs circled by gliding sharks. We took turns complaining about our writing—the instability, clients who wouldn't pay, editors who treated us poorly. As Mary Beth walked ahead of me to the saltwater tropical fish tank, I thought, *You can't die. We hate all the same people.*

After leaving the aquarium, we tromped across the beach to the edge of the tan-foamed surf, our bootheels sinking into the sand, hair blown around by the wind, then dropped onto a boardwalk bench and kept talking. I didn't know if Mary Beth, my Coney Island Baby, would be here in a year, or even in six months. Neither of us could determine when the calendar would flip shut. While we waited to find out, I could let her share her fears about dying, her urgent need to keep some semblance of normalcy in her daughters' lives, and her anger at the random maliciousness of cancer, which had struck not only her but one of her dearest childhood friends. I'd have traveled with Mary Beth to Lourdes for healing water or sought the spinning sun at Medjugorje if it would have helped her get better, but it turned out that the most healing place I could be was right by her side while she talked. Listening is the route to holiness.

At the end of the clinical trial, Mary Beth's tumors shrunk until they disappeared completely. She was among the first in her trial group to become cancer-free, and her combination treatment of Yervoy and Opdivo was approved by the FDA a short time later. But that future was unforeseeable. Only God knew what the plan was then.

What could I bring into that space of unknowing but hot dogs and cheese fries and deep talk? We weren't prophets or miracle workers or even soldiers marching with the army of the blindly devout. We were frightened but faithful optimists, reduced to the message of what we could see. Looming over the abandoned boardwalk, we saw the wire giant of the parachute drop, the Cyclone coaster, the Wonder Wheel stopped for the winter, and circling in the air above us, a hosanna of shrieking gulls.

16

FOXHOLES

When you've been married a while, Valentine's Day becomes a bit like Groundhog Day. Same old glorious same old. I'm too fatigued by crowds for a steak dinner eaten in an aggressively charming bistro with the hordes of other starry-eyed lovers, and what to give to a man's man who doesn't want flowers, jewelry, or chocolates? Never one skilled at crafts—I am a downright menace with a glue gun—I stick to store-bought valentines. After a certain number of years—who knows how many, exactly—it started to feel as though I'd given my beloved the same card over and over again. I tend toward glittered greetings, which make a mess; Mike's hands and Henley sweaters twinkle with the stuff well into the markdown-chocolate days afterward.

What I try to convey, in these cards selected with great care, albeit at the last minute in our local Rite Aid, is that my husband, my brave soldier, is a part of me. Like the love communicated in the e.e. cummings poem that says the most remarkable thing: I carry your heart with me—I carry it in my heart.[1]

Mike and I are both convinced that destiny brought us together on a breezy October day in Brooklyn's Green-Wood Cemetery. He showed up in uniform, looking like Major Healey from the old *I Dream of Jeannie* reruns, while I, in plaid miniskirt, box-heel Mary Janes, and magenta turtleneck, was dressed like a librarian crossed with Daphne from *Scooby-Doo*. Had either of us made any other plan for that day, we'd never have met. "Hand of God," Mike always says. "Hand of God."

Before we met, my presupposition about the faith of soldiers was that they all went to the Church of "Kill 'Em All and Let God Sort 'Em Out." But one of the great lessons always put before me—long before I gave God any credit—is the task of tackling my arrogance. (The Lord sayeth unto thee: get over thyself.) My assumptions are tested more rigorously than my faith.

I took a closer look at Mike, fell in love with who I saw, and by some insane magic, we have been married for almost fifteen years.

I think the secret to lasting love is compliments. That, and marrying someone similar to you in the ways that count, but different enough to keep you interested. A certain amount of dynamic tension keeps it alight.

Beyond our sharing core values and puerile humor, what's kept us together—not forever joined like superglued pennies but more like the stretchy, *boing!*-back adhesive of rubber cement—is the matching of the wills. I know I'd be a disaster with a guy I could dominate, and he'd certainly rear back under a bridle of apron strings. And the hard fact of his faith has been a light in my life.

Mike's religiousness never brought him any trouble but for when a robber snatched his gold Christ head pendant during one of the long morning subway rides from Woodhaven to Stuyvesant High School. When Mike decided to focus his history studies in college, he chose immigration, so loving and welcoming the stranger comes naturally to him. He's a reserved but genial guy, and moving from army post to army post over twenty years lent him an enviable social limberness.

Our love is testimony to the steadying power of faith. There was no concrete proof that I could outrun my demons when Mike and I reunited after our separation, but he chose to believe. He has modeled for me, above anything else, the transformative, lifesaving, and heart-altering power of making the radical choice to go all in. If that were all he had done for me, that would be enough. Constancy is masculine grace made manifest.

Prayer helps, certainly, in keeping the spacecraft in orbit. Even for the petty grievances, it helps to hit your knees. When the baby swiped from the counter and broke yet another pair of my reading glasses—with heavy black Buddy Holly frames that I thought made me look slick—Mike said, "You know, if you got bifocals, you wouldn't have to take them off as often." That night, I prayed the Lord would restrain me from smothering my husband with a pillow—you know, accidentally—while he slept.

We say please and thank you and I'm sorry, even if it's rather belated. But we argue. Oh yes, we do. You hear it said that "a good marriage is one where both partners feel they got the better deal." Know, also, that a good marriage is one where both partners realize that as much as your spouse irritates you, you are also equally irritating. Possibly more.

I am the worst. Despite years of attempted rehabilitation, I'm still an Olympic-grade eye-roller, plus I have the chronic problem of cutting Mike off when I think he's taking too long to make a point.

"Oh, I'm sorry," he says when I do this. "Was I talking while you were interrupting?"

A long marriage is a minuet of care. I'd completely recovered from the difficult birth, but Mike, already tired from the late nights stumbling to and from the nursery, started feeling worse—fatigued, with aching joints and brain fog. We worried that his Lyme disease was coming back. He'd been diagnosed two years earlier when mysterious red patches bloomed up on his back during a trip to Key West. With no Lyme-bearing ticks in Florida, the physicians at the Lower Keys Medical Center were so unfamiliar with Lyme they had to Google the symptoms. He explained that he likes to jog on a heavily wooded river trail rife with ticks, and he had every symptom on the list. They sent him home with three weeks' worth of doxycycline, and he was fine. Until now.

Dutchess County, New York, where we live, is the ground zero of Lyme disease, with the highest concentration of cases in the entire country. A local infectious disease specialist sent Mike to the hospital for a spinal tap to see if the Lyme spirochetes had moved into his neurological system, causing his distress—including the mental fogginess, a little-known symptom of advanced Lyme. At its most extreme, Lyme can have fatal complications.

In the hospital waiting room, I dandled the baby on my knee in her pink panda bear sweater set and counted the colored tiles in the hallway floor pattern. Then I rolled her back and forth in her Sherman tank stroller.

Mike had had a life-threatening neurological disease as a child, so severe that the elderly priest from their Woodhaven parish shook out the holy water and administered last rites over his paralyzed fourteen-year-old body. Any disease involving spinal fluid makes me very nervous. My depression, my traumatic birth, now this. Here we were, again, at "in sickness and in health."

The nurse in SpongeBob SquarePants scrubs cheerfully led me and the baby to the recovery ward where she yanked back the thin pastel-print curtain on its metal track. Mike was already hooked up to his first intravenous treatment, but he waved me and the baby over. He pulled the happy fatso onto his lap, arranging his wires and tubes around her. The Lyme titers were maxed out, and the only way to kill the bugs in his system was heavy, chemo-dose antibiotics administered through a PICC line, which ran (and here I swooned, the room tilting, as the doctor explained) through a vein up his arm and all the way into his heart. My sweet husband would become, essentially, host to a dedicated pipeline for pharmaceuticals. The nuclear option.

With the PICC line installed, Mike sat at our kitchen island, slowly injecting the drugs into the port that led to his bloodstream. I saw this as a grisly opportunity for gratitude. I hated that war had taken 50 percent of his hearing, that it had separated him from his family (he'd missed the birth of his first son during Desert Storm), and that I'd always worry about the long-term effects of the many Army-mandated vaccines he'd been given, as well as certain anxieties that trouble a combat veteran's heart. But his military service gave us consistent, quality health insurance. For his sacrifice, he would never have to go begging for medical care. Lose some, yes, but win some too.

For this, and so many other mixed-bag blessings, I'm not among the fair-weather faithful. Through the breakdowns, the traumas, the illnesses, and the losses, it is sometimes difficult to hold on to God. But faith is a more secure foxhole than fear. I remember that the root word of *salvation* is *salvus*, meaning "safe." I can grab on to that invisible hand. I can shift from *This crap never ends* to *This, too, shall pass.*

Sometimes the best I can squeeze in is a prayer on the fly. A pause, if not for reflection then for begging my better angels to stay on the job and not abandon me in my fretting and frantic lunacy. Giving it up to God when you're overwhelmed looks a lot like tossing a cartoon bomb with a sparking wick at the sky, shouting "Here, this is going to detonate any second. Would you mind?"

I know enough soldiers to affirm that, yes, there are atheists in foxholes, but not in this one.

Mike and I take turns doing daycare drop-off—I usually do mornings, then he picks up the baby after he leaves work. There is a soldier whose older son is in the classroom next to our daughter's. I pass the soldier as we wrangle our kids, him frequently carrying two in his arms at once. You can't tell from his gait that he had a leg amputated above the knee; you only know when he wears his PT shorts—the ultramodern prosthetic limb clearly visible. On the back of the calf of his untouched leg is a tattoo of the word *Heart* inked in bold letters underneath. Military culture has shown me that as inspiration uplifts, it often humbles too.

I still liked our baby a lot—as she started walking and talking, her personality emerged. She was half Felix Unger, half primal fire. Like the Great Universal Toddler, she wanted what she wanted when she wanted it, and what she didn't want to do, she fought. Hard. Changing diapers and putting on socks and shoes were a battle royale. I was astonished at how her mood dictated the course of a given day—Pol Pot in a onesie.

The workaday stress of toddlerdom was wearing out Mike and me. She slept well, but her tantrums competed against the ticking clock of her early daycare drop-off. This made us edgy, especially when she thrashed around socking whatever was easy to hit. Usually one of us.

Around the planet, millions of partners in parenting face identical stress every day, but it's hard to maintain perspective when a thirty-four-pound virago is punching you in the chin and kicking her meaty little feet at your shins as the car idles in the garage.

As Mike tried to jam a shoe onto her flailing foot, *Daniel Tiger's Neighborhood* already playing on the seat-back iPad, he said, "If you keep hitting people, one of these days someone's going to hit you back."

What he meant was that if she hits another kid, the kid might give her a swat in response.

I misinterpreted what he said as: if she hits daddy again, daddy will hit her.

The fire came from the deepest, most survival-bound depths of my reptilian brain, where rage is my default. I reared back. "Get out. Get out. *Get out!*"

"Excuse me?"

This is what being triggered is like: the emotion comes flaming out, a split-second reflex faster than any rational response, a reaction based in pure survival instinct. The alarm has sounded—*Danger, danger!*—and anyone in the immediate vicinity is hosed. Trauma dwells in a different part of the brain than memory—someplace faster to alert, that sets off all the warning flares at once.

There was no God for me in that moment. Only fear. Or maybe fear, underneath it all, was my God. My being had been an altar to fear since I can't remember when.

I stormed up the stairs.

Mike came up right after me, carrying the baby. "Did you just tell me to get out?"

"Yes," I hissed. "I told you to get out."

The baby reached for me, so Mike handed her over. With the baby in my arms, I said, "If you ever hit her, I'll have you arrested."

He was furious. Who wouldn't be, when greeted with a good-morning message of "I think you're really a child abuser"?

He left for work. My nerves settled, the tide of molten lava subsided, and I texted apology after apology. I picked up my phone when finally it buzzed against the glass top of my nightstand. He'd typed a single sentence: "You've known me for sixteen years and I still haven't gained your trust." One of those poison-dart texts that easily finds its target—the old ticker.

I don't want to be the woman who needs to flee to the therapist on the regular. I hate apportioning so many hours to staying sane, and, frankly, I'd rather be throwing money at movie tickets for Mike and me, and mocha lattes and, you know, college savings for our daughter. But with rage like that bursting out of nowhere, bringing in the explosive ordnance disposal specialist is what must be done. It's part of my routine care, like people who require dialysis, physical therapy, or blood sugar monitoring. Sometimes you need your prescription changed, your perspective shifted. Being healthy meant more time in the talking chair—life and limb and holy matrimony depended on it. You don't simply decide to live without fear—you have to cut the trip wires. That's how you heal post-traumatic stress. You defuse it.

Your history, the various struggles of your life—they're all packed away inside you somewhere. You are everything that ever happened to you. Which super-sucks when your complicated past explodes into the present. In the panic of misunderstanding, my loving husband had been redrawn and recast as another creepy guy, a threat to children, seen through the eyes of the threatened child I was. As writer and mental health advocate Yolo Akili Robinson says, some of us don't recreate chaos and dysfunction because it's what we want. Some of us create it because it's all we know.[2]

My husband has a Legion of Merit medal, handed over to him with great flourish in a green velvet clamshell box the day he retired after twenty-one years of military service. He stowed it in a plastic chest of slide-out drawers full of junk in the basement. There's also a drawer containing photos of him in every phase of his military career, from baby-faced at basic training to his final promotion, his mother pinning the silver oak leaf Lieutenant Colonel rank to his epaulets. He doesn't display any of these things at home. He doesn't covet attention—no spotlight Ranger, he. His accomplishments are racked up same as anyone in the armed services: he doesn't do something for the applause; he does something because he knows it's right. Like every soldier I know, he doesn't want to be called a hero. He just wants to be called a good man.

The duties most vital to maintaining long-term love are these: choosing your battles and counting your blessings. I do view my husband as my battle buddy in this war called "you and me against the world." We're a united front.

No, we don't shoot out the lights on Valentine's Day with wine and rose petals trailing down the hall. We do store-bought cards and slow dances and sweet kisses. While we don't advertise our victories, they're there. He may have rigid attachment to routine, but he'll loosen his laces to accommodate me. He's on my side. And I'm on his. I don't always trust, but I always try. And that, as cummings himself might say, is the wonder that's keeping the stars apart. I carry my husband's heart with me. I carry it in the foxhole I carry in my heart.

17

FRUITFUL

The sun rose on my first Mother's Day in rays of confetti colors. I loved the breakfast in bed, the Mason jar full of daisies, the rye toast with singed edges, and orange juice sloshing over the edge of the cup on the wobbly tray. I loved the baby's little pink paint handprint on the "I love you, Mommy!" potholder she made at daycare. I tacked it up on my office bulletin board, where it will stay even if the house should fall down around me.

I even loved the feeling of harried unity with the other mothers the Friday before the holiday as I walked the corridors of the West Point daycare center—the hurried steps and the winces of guilt as the babies wailed when we hustled out of the rooms after drop-off. Our eyes would meet in recognition and we'd smile at one another—*been there.* Whether we showed up in work-at-home jeans and sweatshirts or camouflage uniforms and tan suede desert boots, hair twisted and pinned up over the collar, Army regulation–style, we were all in it together. I also loved the daycare workers who took my baby from me and sat her down to Cheerios and cling peaches with the other kids, for they, in my absence, mothered my child too.

Given how much we're told motherhood changes women—makes us more sensitive, compassionate, caring, and connected to the world, imagine my surprise when I realized during that first year that I wasn't radically transformed. I was just me, with a kid.

For most of my life, I never wanted kids. Now I had a funny, observant, affectionate baby daughter, and sometimes I still didn't want kids. But I learned to separate my frustrations with the slog of parenting from my actual child. I think I'll keep her. But that doesn't mean I'm in a hurry to foist parenting upon anyone else. Some women eschew parenting until the biological clock goes off, then they're singing the praises of Mommy and Me classes and Mustela lotion and homemade sweet potato puree to any woman who will listen—even those who've said they don't want children a million times, and still mean it. *Momzilla attacks!* But the impulse to reform eluded me. Where motherhood is concerned, I am not in the sales business.

I know the Bible says to be fruitful and multiply. If we're keeping score of Scripture verse used as chastening rod—and I am the type who's always keeping score about *something*—this one ranks near the top of the list. We are so invested in the idea of having kids as the ultimate path to fulfillment; to deepest, most authentic contribution; to really and truly and deeply *adult,* as a verb.

Meanwhile, Barbara, My Sister the Minister, who doesn't have children, has worked her entire adult life on behalf of the young and the vulnerable. Prior to entering seminary, she worked to mobilize a boycott of major corporations that were selling diluted infant formula in Third World countries. Even now, on top of being pastor of a sizable congregation, she stops by the local McDonald's one day a week, sitting there with a Styrofoam cup of coffee, offering free prayers and a listening ear as her own extracurricular "McMinistry." My sister may be so distractible that she'd lose her knitting needles in a pup tent, but she's good at her job, and people instinctively open their hearts to her.

Now what were we saying about motherhood as the ultimate contribution?

I love my child. I like my child. I would die for my child a thousand times. But I can't sign on to the idea that the most authentic love in the universe is the love a parent has for a child, or that mothers are morally superior. Or that a parent even automatically loves a child— we've all seen cases where that's not true. And some of the most loving, engaged, and joyful people I know are childless. I've been brilliantly nurtured by women who can't even keep a houseplant alive. I'll take someone realistic about their interests over a self-obsessed procreator any old day.

The notion of maternal supremacy is one of the great whispered-behind-the-hand cruelties. It is a slap in the face to women who have everything to offer except the mom credential, men with innate caretaking prowess, and children waiting in vain for the loving mother they've been promised, who then exhaust themselves trying to court her appearance well into their own adulthoods.

Most of all, it is an insult to every woman everywhere to suggest that she must wait, like the Velveteen Rabbit, until she has the love of a child to become real. Some women choose not to be mothers; some have that choice made for them by circumstances that would hurt you greatly to hear. And some women aren't cut out to care for others as their primary focus—they are meant, instead, to be occupied and defined by their art or journeying or lifelong uninterrupted study. One woman's destiny may be the nursery; another woman's, the library. Still another's, the laboratory.

My own mother never pressured any of her children to become parents. When I was in my early twenties, she'd told me she wasn't sure she'd have had children if she felt she had a choice—getting married and having kids was just what women did back then, she said. Before we came along, she painted as a hobby. She was quite a gifted watercolorist, but five children ate up all her time, and the paint box and brushes were put away. My father kept a few of her watercolors in his top dresser drawer. Oh, the sad symbolism—they were all paintings of fruit.

My mother came to our house to meet the baby after she was born, parking her Irish walking stick—a tag on the leather strap saying, "Not all who wander are lost"—by the front door. Spinal stenosis had reshaped her from a five-foot-eight ramrod to a five-foot-three-inch question mark. My sister Annette, the dutiful, accommodating middle child, helped lower her into a living room chair so the baby could nest in her arms. The baby reached up to touch my mother's face and curled her tiny hand around her pointer finger.

The trust and affection between them carried a sweet ache along with it. I would never experience that innocent, bare vulnerability with my mother. Maybe sometimes love has to skip a generation to be pure.

By the time my first Mother's Day rolled around, Annette was already long established as my mother's champion and her medical advocate. Old age involves a ton of paperwork, so, on my mother's behalf, Annette clicked on the green banker's lamp, adjusted her leather visor, and got to work, assembling a cast of doctors, specialists, and physical therapists so large and carefully choreographed it rivaled a Busby Berkeley musical. Annette managed a never-ending gauntlet of appointments, punctuated by surprise visits to the emergency room.

Kelly, one year younger and the Thing 2 to Annette's Thing 1, took over as the legal eagle, making sure Mom kept her accounts current and her affairs in order. She applied her logistician's mind to the business of keeping Mom out of any kind of legal or financial trouble. She packed up and moved from San Diego to Washington, DC, to be closer to family, bringing with her the special sunshine of her laugh and a crate of stuffed animals for the baby, including a plush pink abominable snowman that the baby shrieked at before burying her face in its fur for a hug.

By comparison, my days were easy—dunking the baby in sudsy tubs with floating rubber ducks, helping her take her first bites of mushed avocado and pureed squash, being greeted by her gummy smiles when I picked her up at daycare. The type of caretaking that Annette and Kelly were doing—looking after the old, infirm, and cranky—doesn't come with cuddles and never gets enough credit. Not surprisingly, it is by overwhelming majority women who find themselves taking on, or being tasked with, this role.

After too many falls and too many trips to the emergency room, Mom had to go into assisted living, which she hated. She didn't like the lack of autonomy, the lack of privacy, or the food. The nursing staff told us that since Mom wasn't eating, she'd have to either have a feeding tube surgically implanted or slowly starve. Painful, dangerous surgery or starvation—the Sophie's choice of gastroenterology. With her options laid out before her, Mom started eating again, a little.

Annette faced these types of responsibilities on top of her full-time job as a chemist with an hour-long commute, nearly every day. Felt-tip pen in hand, she wrote out neat scrolls of notes on yellow lined legal pads. She has a head for data and record-keeping. If motherhood is sacrifice and care and protection and love, then I'd say without a hint of exaggeration that my sister is a better mother than I am. Who knows the truest depth of love? Who has given more in the name of family? She tended to an ornery, deteriorating woman with no special day, let alone a card or flower bouquet or candy box for thanks. In light of her workload, my basking in the babbling glow of an adorable baby was no hardship. My sister Annette isn't a mother, but she was doing a heroine's job of parenting our mom at what was so obviously the beginning of the end of her life, giving in a way that I, baby on hip, could not.

At noon on Mother's Day, I dressed the baby in a red and blue Scandinavian print dress, navy blue canvas Mary Janes, and red polka-dot socks and took her to see my mom in the nursing home. Mom lay in her cranked-up bed, barely verbal with a surgical mask over her face to keep the baby from catching her cold. She hadn't been allowed to smoke in months, so her skin was pink, her cheeks plump. But the tininess of her dwindling form against the sheets, which were bleached as thin and blue-white as skim milk, shook me.

Mike was always so kind to my mother, even though he had witnessed her verbal swordplay with me. Now, she was too weak to talk, let alone insult me. He told her about his work, what the baby had been trying to say most recently—*hi, dada, ma*. She lay still, her grey hair long and fanned behind her on the pillow, her eyes tracking the baby as I carried her back and forth alongside the bed. Mom was tired, so our visit was kept short.

After the canned and static feel of the nursing home, we needed green grass and a cleansing breeze. At home, Mike and I rolled around with the baby in the backyard, afternoon sun turning the white siding on our house a bronzy orange. I lay on the lawn, and she grabbed on to me to pull herself to standing, grinning with pride. Cruising along my side, she leaned over to Mike and started clapping her hands on his cheeks, like an Italian *nonna* crying, *"Che faccia bello!"* The great privilege of mothering is watching a child grow—into her body, her personality, and the larger world. If mothering has changed me in one significant way, it is that I'm rooted in purpose—to break the cycle of maternal shortcoming. Everything else around me might shift, shrink, or disappear completely, but my daughter and I belong to each other, for keeps. Yet there are so many other ways to ground yourself, countless ways to bear fruit, many methods of healing.

When the baby was just born, Annette gave the baby a set of yellow children's sized gardening tools in a canvas tote bag shaped like a turtle, with green webbing handles looping from its back. To be fruitful is to bring something to beneficence—anything. Flowers. Stories. Songs. Friendships. Annette's real gift of fruition shows up in her gardening, begetting beautiful abundance—colorful things. Edible things. Lupine and milkweed to host butterflies, fragrant basil and mint potted on shelves, and tomatoes and zucchini in such quantity, she donates the basket-brimming excess to the food bank in brown paper grocery sacks.

Annette is going to teach the baby to plant daffodils. Our mother's favorite. In the fall, she'll dig the holes in our backyard soil and the baby will drop in the amber-skinned bulbs to sleep through the winter. Then, by April, we'll have so many flowers. When they burst into bloom, waving in the spring rain like a riot of skinny girls in yellow raincoats, they'll look really pretty. I can already see Annette and the baby cutting a few together, Annette guiding the snip of the shear, then filling the Mason jar with water and setting it on the kitchen windowsill, the flowers the fruit of their bond.

18

⁜

STUFF

The first rule of Hoarders' Kids Club is you don't talk about being a hoarder's kid. I guess I'm free to talk about it now, though, because she's gone. My mom is gone. She died. A statement so huge, so sad, so liberating and devastating, I can scarcely wrap my head around it. Still.

Understand, of course, that my mother wasn't a *hoarder*. No. She was a pack rat. That's the prevailing story, one that all five of us kids told with increased repetition and emphasis as the years passed and the condition worsened. Every family has its fictions, stories held together by strings and sticky tape. Scraps of paper onto which certain words are scribbled, then obeyed as if inked on parchment, a royal decree. Words that become their own toxic gospel.

The words on the scraps in my family's messy paper heap? In my mother's tiny, pretty lettering:

"It could be worse."

"It's just stuff."

"I need some company, then I can start sorting."

And voiced, in the most artificially offhanded way my mother could muster, "My wants are many, my needs are few."

That expression, with its combined finality and futility, started the Cold War in my family, all of us squaring off against this mental impairment that would prove bigger than any of us. Even as a united front of five kids, each gently wheedling and supporting in our way after our dad died, we watched her disappear under piles and racks and bags and boxes of stuff.

My mother was no housekeeper, and she didn't require that we compensate for her deficit. I didn't make my bed regularly until I was in my thirties; I've left more than my share of dirty dishes to grow fuzzy in my kitchen sink. I learned my domesticity the hard way: by marrying someone who is so fastidious and order-driven, he's distracted if there are clothes draped on the back of the bedroom chair. In the name of domestic harmony I fell in line, growing neater each year, until one day at age forty, I surprised myself by using the word *tidy* as a qualifier to describe myself. Whipping your housekeeping skills into shape to please a man isn't feminist, but it worked, and I'm for whatever works.

Mom was messy everywhere we set up camp. In Pennsylvania, piles of dirty laundry mounded up along the stairway bannister in the upstairs hallway. When we lived in Michigan and my brother went away to college, his bedroom became the "junk room," which is to say, utterly impassible. The force and velocity of the messiness increased over time to verifiable pathology by the time I was a teenager. Our house in New Jersey—a dank, brown, split-level housing development affair that we all hated—became her hoardering haven.

By eighth grade, I was the only kid living under my parents' roof. Mom started shopping more and more, and as the bedrooms emptied, the clothing piles increased. The tumble of purchases stacked everywhere included countless pairs of third-markdown sneakers from Marshall's, still in the box; scarves; turtlenecks; and long, shapeless, loose-weave sweaters she loved, all piled up three-feet deep on the vacant twin beds. On a dresser top was an Ouroboros-like snarl of inexpensive belts, woven metallic gold pleather, canvas web in bright, preppy colors with metal D-ring loops. The majority she would never wear. She paid full price for none of it.

Hoarders often present well in public. My mother had impeccable penmanship, remembered birthdays, and kept appointments. She went to the doctor, even if she ignored the medical advice, particularly to quit smoking. Every time my mother got out of her car—a yellow VW Beetle which I meanly nicknamed "the Clutter Bug," crammed as it was with cigarette wrappers, magazines, books, shopping bags, smelly old blackened banana peels, and food wrappers, all plainly visible to passersby—she'd look in the rearview mirror, smooth down her hair, and put on lipstick.

A song I love says we're all one phone call from our knees. My uncle Harvey, my mom's younger brother and her foil in housekeeping disaster, had never had to snap into form to care for anyone. No wife, no kids, no partner, no roommate. He lived in my grandmother's modest house in North Baltimore, a shaggy dog dining out on Social

Security checks and a modest inheritance. I hadn't seen him in six years—he wasn't up for visitors—though we talked often enough for me to agree to be the executor of his estate when the time came. The unwritten agreement was that I would be the caretaker too.

With no family nearby, Uncle Harvey's care fell to his friends. Rich, one of his writing group buddies, dropped by a couple times a week with groceries and whatever else he needed. One day when Harvey's cell phone went unanswered, Rich went over to check on him. No answer when he knocked. He couldn't get the door to the house open, so he called the paramedics, who broke down the door and found Harvey collapsed amid the mess in his living room, severely dehydrated and near death. They rushed my uncle to the ICU, and when my mother called with the news, I told her I'd head down to Baltimore with my brother Tad to see him, and to see what, if anything, needed to be done with Harvey's house.

It turned out that compared to Harvey, my mom's hoarding was amateur. The reason Rich hadn't been able to get the door open was because it was blocked by mounds of trash in the kitchen. Years' worth of mail piled up under the slot in the front door had socked in that entrance too. When Tad and I entered, we plugged our noses against the stench—rotten food, mildew, God knows what. We climbed over the trash mountain in the kitchen, then skidded on an ankle-deep drift of empty red Chips Ahoy! bags and Dr Pepper bottles in the living room. Normally chatty, my brother and I were speechless at the sight before us. Filth on every surface. Paint peeled from the ceiling, hanging in great sheets, black mold curling the edges among the dust-greyed cobwebs that hung, haunted-house style, low enough to skim your hair.

We picked, slid, and kicked our way through the mess in shock. Tad did the one thing he knew how to do: He put a technological device between him and the situation. He started snapping photos of the mess with his phone. As we moved from room to room, or tried to, shaking our heads, I snarled, "You'd better not show these to Mom!"

In the ICU, Harvey had been shaved, medicated, stabilized, and fed better than I'm sure he had been in months. It was hard to see him, wild-eyed and disoriented in his hospital bed. But not as hard as seeing this house. This was the house my frugal, hardworking grandmother bought in the 1950s and kept neat as a pin until her death.

Tad left the following morning, and I started calling cleaning services. The power of denial allowed me to dismiss one $10,000 bid, quoted due to the house being a biohazard site, and I settled on four kids in a SERVPRO van. I forwarded the significantly lower bid to my mom, who approved it. Mom appreciated expediency and excellence, and I knew it, having made a lifetime of performing like a ball-balancing seal to win her favor. I lined up the cleaning crew and sprung into action. Here was my shot to be a star gleaming in her eye once again.

The Dumpster showed up in the morning, the green SERVPRO van shortly after, and we took up sixty-gallon black plastic garbage bags and went to work. For several hours, the crew dug in—actually dug in, with shovels—the Baltimore heat sending rivulets of sweat down their smooth brows and strong backs.

I sorted and sifted, pulling trash from treasure. In some irrational part of my mind, I thought I'd better hurry or Harvey might come home and stop me. But as the sun rose higher and the house heated up in the late spring weather, I muscled in. The exhilaration of being able to throw things out with impunity pushed me forth. I salvaged what I could: a pretty Alexander Calder print, a pop art poster in a sunshine yellow metal frame, my grandmother's wedding band from her second husband. I could've sat outside on the concrete steps, drinking my Snapple and watching the overgrown hostas along the front walk nod in the breeze, and let the guys carry everything away. Call it all scrap. But that felt like an insult. He'd had good taste once.

I loved the SERVPRO crew—they didn't make a peep of judgment or disgust. They shoveled, bagged, scrubbed, and schlepped with their healthy twentysomething arms. They didn't care that the old, loose basement tiles were full of asbestos, but they didn't want to touch the Ouija board they found in a damp corner—too creepy for these nice Southern souls. I grabbed it in my gloved hands and flung it into the Dumpster. *Get thee behind me, Satan!* No problem.

Harvey wasn't home to know what was going on, but I still wished for a way to conceal this disaster scene from the neighbors to spare his dignity. Fear of visibility is a huge part of the disorder's negative impact. The mess on the outside reflects the mess on the inside, and the shame it causes is acute. But there was no way to hide what was going on. What he'd wanted hidden was being hefted into a Dumpster parked on the street in broad daylight.

The neighbors gathered. A woman walking a small dog stopped to watch with the man who lived in a handsome little colonial next door. "Hey," she said. "Your uncle could be on that show!"

I am familiar with that show: *Hoarders.* I can't watch it without getting a bad case of trigger-nerves. The frantic look in the subject's eyes when an expert comes in and tries to organize things, the tears as the stuff is hauled away. *Don't fix the mess,* I thought the one time I shuddered through a whole episode. *Fix the disordered brain and the frenetic heart it breaks.* When someone you love, someone with whom you are entangled, is spectacle-level sick, it is hard not to snap a protective arm around them and their whole sad, spectacular mess.

I wasn't brave enough to do the deep detective work, to go all forensic investigator on my uncle's condition with the doctors. How long was his hair when they found him? Was it matted and stained with smoke? Had he soiled himself? The home's one bathroom was walled off behind a hip-high pile of trash, so how did he take care of the basics? Or did he simply not? Based on the evidence, I knew there was no answer I'd be able to withstand.

This was the worst-case scenario envisioned by anyone who loves a hoarder: that they'd collapse in, or under, a pile of crap. But thanks to his friend Rich, he was still alive, though barely. I may not believe in wing-and-harp angels, but I believe Rich was as close to a guardian angel as my uncle was likely to get.

My uncle. My quirky, brilliant, bookish uncle who merged the suave of George Plimpton with the loopiness of the Absent-Minded Professor. Always in a tweed cap, button-down shirt, suede patch blazer, and jeans that made him look dapper. He never nailed it down with a partner, kids, or much of a career, but he excelled at friendship. Because of him, I got to sit in the famous home library of his friend, Johns Hopkins professor Dick Macksey, where I touched a genuine Gutenburg Bible then sat in his kitchen pretending to sip port—which I've always hated—while they spoke of seeing Babe Ruth play baseball when they were kids. Now he was in an ICU, soon to be shipped to a nursing home, never to return to that house. Never to know what became of all his stuff.

There will forever be a spot in my heart that aches with shortcoming around my uncle. Why didn't we do something? Why didn't we do more? But the immutable truth is he shut his door against us long ago—my sister Kelly tried to visit him in 2005 and he wouldn't even come to the porch to wave hello—and the door only opened again when it was pried from its hinges by paramedics. He died alone fourteen months later.

Some people spin beyond your reach, and if the angels know why, they aren't telling.

As Mom's hoarding problem worsened, our complicity was sealed one sad look and shrug at a time. None of us said anything to her or to one another. Periodically my dad would take a valiant stab at a pile—the stack of old plastic dishes and cups lining the kitchen counter covered in dust and potting soil, or the blizzard drifts of paper on the kitchen desk, but whatever progress was made would be undone within weeks, if not days. Our old grouchy calico, a stray we took in when she showed up at our door pregnant, became rebellious about relieving herself as she aged, and the basement became, and remained, a vast, linoleum-tiled litter box. Whenever I visited their house, I shut the door and ignored it.

It took putting a continent between Mom and us for the truth to be faced squarely. Annette and I met at the Newark airport to fly to San Diego for a sisters' weekend. Somehow, we ended up referencing the Mount Olympus of laundry in the mudroom. Annette told me she'd dropped by one day to help Dad try to dig through the clothes and sort them, rewashing what had become soiled again by sitting for so long. "I was digging through the laundry in front of the washer and when I got to the bottom of the pile, I found a snakeskin. An empty snakeskin."

The clothes had sat there long enough to not only house a snake, but to house a snake for so long, it was able to nest, shed its skin, and move on. The grotesque absurdity burst the bubble of denial as graphically as a blood blister popping. Not only was our mom's problem as bad as I thought, it was worse. Annette had noticed and dared to say something. Now I had a witness.

My sister, blessed with a natural equanimity and poise, smiled right along with me as I laughed. And laughed. The sole occasion when I actually laughed until I cried.

They're called *pack rats* or *clutterbugs*, and the narrow paths that wind between the piles of junk are called *goat trails*. These are the cutesy linguistics of chaos, a way of drawing an adorable, marching animal cracker border around an ever-expanding problem. Papers, books, clothes, dishes, trash—whatever threatens to spill over its boundary and into open space. The cuddly language does nothing to facilitate discussion about the issue. Hoarders carry with them an exaggerated air of fragility, laced with chronic agitation. Their demeanor is so brittle that it seems the mere acknowledgment of the affliction will shatter them into a million pieces. Ah, the irony: this would create yet more mess to clean.

The families of hoarders become expert at edging carefully around the elephant in the room. And the pile of old *Women's Day* magazines. And seasonal decorating supplies. And bottles of expired medicine. And shoes. And empty jars and cans. The survival of the hoarder parent, or, more covertly expressed, the survival of the parent's regard for you, depends on your discretion. Shine a light on this disaster scene, and the burden of guilt shifts to you.

Estimates run high. One of every fifty people may be a hoarder[1]— and yet we all think we're the only one with a hoarding parent, living apart in these shallows of isolation. We soak it up alone, never aware that a few sandbars over, there are more shallows, with yet more briny, lonely residents.

Meanwhile, all we notice are the people around us who don't understand. Outsiders, many well-meaning, see your strings being pulled, and they can't see why you don't just cut them. Because somewhere in there, inside the grown-up kid, is the little kid with the single, irrational wish that if she did the right thing, this could turn out differently. Her actions could somehow fix the broken parent, if only she knew the right thing to do. That's what keeps her tied in place: that wondering and hoping and wanting. For good or ill, there is no force stronger than love. Except, perhaps, for wishful thinking.

Here's where friends speak up, making you shiver in your little shell: *Well*, they say, *why don't you get in there and help them clean? Send a maid over!* This is where every hoarder's kid blushes, freezes with a sputter, stares down at the ground, or laughs darkly, burrowing a little further into the sand.

As advice, *send a maid over* makes about as much sense as pouring your dear boozy aunt's Shiraz down the drain. Managing people's symptoms for them is not solving their problems or even an effective step toward it. Action without proven efficacy is just superstitious ritual. May as well ensure your immortality by whistling past a graveyard.

The heartbreak of hoarders is that they're broken, and most of them know it. Something in the decision-making metric of the brain isn't firing right. It's a neighboring branch to OCD, but not quite that. They can't see their way around to dealing with all that stuff—*I might need it! But I want it! I'm too tired to sort it! But I paid so much for it! I'd better keep it.* And around and around and around. In my mom's case, she'd get frustrated that she couldn't focus enough to get the mess to budge—shame and analysis-paralysis locked in embrace—and we'd get frustrated with her. Then, I'd feel guilty for getting mad: *How could you? Don't you get it?*

This wasn't laziness or a lifestyle choice. She was *sick*.

The lack of practical knowledge for managing hoarding will make you crazy on its own. Is it like substance abuse, where the person has to curtail the behavior while loved ones refuse to enable it? Do we jump in and help, knowing that the hoard will only re-appear? Does medication work? I would have done anything if only I'd known what to do. If only.

But when I don't know what to do? Despair. Then prayer.

I'd come far enough to trust that I could ask, and reasonably expect, guidance from God, which had been unthinkable for so long. I believed now that someone would come on the line when I called—someone whose ideas were reliably better than my own best thinking. The answer I got back from the prayer of *What do I do?* was *Do what you can*. Which was next to nothing.

I knew that trying to clean my mom's house would set off her anxiety, which would likely set off a verbal barb that would leave me quivering for days. So occasionally, I'd drop in for a visit, stopping first at the convenience store next door for reinforcements. One time, as I filled up a thirty-two-ounce cup with Diet Coke, I found myself thinking about how scientists can grow a whole liver out of a half in a petri dish. Pick your poison. Diet soda is mine.

I never lasted long on these visits to Mom's place. The mess made me nervous, and the smoke and dust made me wheeze. I'd leave within a couple of hours, wound up like a cuckoo clock, wondering why I couldn't get it together to pal around with my mom, to keep a lonely old woman company. Then, on the drive home, as if by magic,

I'd remember one of her famous zingers that would keep me away for months.

There is no one on earth who can wound with words like a mother. I wished I could let it all go, but while my mind and heart were willing, my body said no go. As a young child, I'd cry if I were apart from her. Now I could hardly stand to be near her. I'd get stomachaches if I was with her for too long. My mother loved quoting that old saw, "Of course I push your buttons. I installed them." The truth about mothers is they never comprehend the true extent of their reach.

I think a lot about how to keep the channel clear with my daughter. Mothers and daughters. Daughters and their moms. It's so complex. I can't help but remember the pre-adoption workplace inspection episode of *30 Rock*, when Tina Fey as Liz Lemon, who is hoping she'll be approved to adopt a baby, cradles a little prop doll and says to her coworker, "Is it so wrong that I just want to have one of these to grow up and resent me?"[2] While I would love a peaceful, supportive relationship with my own daughter, let's just say I know the odds here.

If God offers us a hand to hold in troubled times, God also offers a nice, firm shove when the situation requires. Did you ever get that cosmic shove, where you're jolted out of place by forces you can't explain, as if being shaken awake? Whether it was prescience, or the aggressive edge of grace, when Annette called to tell me in January that Mom wasn't doing well, the message from the woo-woo zone was clear: dress the baby in something cute, pack up Mike, and go.

Mom was in her nursing home bed, yoked to tube and cords, a two-prong plastic plug gently blowing oxygen into her nose. She lay shrunken against the mattress, in and out of awareness. She saw the baby and smiled, then her eyelids fluttered shut and she started pulling away as if to sleep. I remembered when the baby first met her, how the baby reached up with both hands from the pillow on my mom's lap and grabbed her face. How a few weeks ago during our Christmas visit to the home, the baby blew her a kiss, which she never did for anyone.

Mom didn't look great. Her eyes opened and closed, her hand now and then rising up and jerking as if tensing under an electric current. Machines around her pinged and clicked, like clocks on countdown. I knew it as I was seeing it. *She's dying. She's dying.*

We did not make the good-bye formal. She fell asleep, and we left without waking her.

The ride home, whizzing along the Jersey daredevil eight-lane highways, was tense and exhausting. In the passenger seat, I didn't pray so much as seethe in reproach: "God, why do you continue to let her suffer? If you're this entity of infinite mercy, allegedly, where are you now? Why prolong this misery? What gives?" Each syllable of this rant-as-prayer was expressed as sharply as a finger poked in that broad, galactic chest.

At home, I sulked and raged my way through a hot bath in hopes of chasing sleep. No luck. I was so angry at God, angrier than I had ever been, and that's saying something. I didn't know why a merciful God would be such a sadist.

I also didn't know that the baby had somehow disconnected the answering machine, so incoming calls were going straight to a voice-mail box. My sister had called around midnight, and the voicemail caught the call so I didn't have to hear her say directly to me that our mother had died. Her heart, it seemed, simply gave out.

I thought about God and the tirade I'd unleashed on him for the past several hours. What did I have to say for myself now?

Before I went upstairs to wake Mike to tell him, I sat at the kitchen counter, steepled my fingers, and bowed my head for a second. *Thanks. For the relief. For the mercy. For the reminder that you're up there doing your job.*

With Mom gone, reeled back in by God and rescued from that prison of her declining body, things got easier and they got harder. Warren Buffet cried when his emotionally abusive mother died, not because he was sad, but, as he said, "because of the waste."[3]

At the sidelines of a declining, dysfunctional parent is a child saying, "This is my fault. What is wrong with me that I can't make this work? That I can't make them better?" Nowhere around is some wise, gentle adult, possibly located at a helpful distance from the disaster, to remind you with great tenderness that you are a child, not a sorcerer.

What to make of that overwhelming sense that there's always something more you could've done? Why do we feel as though we come up short in the face of deficiencies that aren't our fault?

Always scared of being verbally attacked by my mom when she was in her stingray mode, I drifted away from her more and more over time, but we always shared the big news: job changes, family developments, anything that might make her proud, even if I ended up getting stung before hanging up. Oddly, after she died, I still had that reflex. I kept wanting to call my mom to tell her that my mom died.

My friend, who finally cut ties with her narcissist mother after being struck in the face in plain view of her six-year-old twin daughters, lamented not being able to have a relationship. Her mother provided daycare while she worked and was crazy about her granddaughters. But my friend knew that for her heart's sake, for her daughters' sake, she had to maintain her distance. No matter how good it may be for a while, the storm clouds would drag in overhead. She said through tears on the phone, because she knew that I'd understand, "My mom is the dog who bites."

When you cut off contact with the woman who raised you, who gave you life, it's a move so radical to some, you might as well be describing self-amputation. "But she's your *mother*. Don't you *love* her?" I don't think they get how desperately we love our mothers. Or the idea of our mothers. Or the idea of perfect mother-love. We chase that dream all our lives. If we're lucky, we fill that loss in healthy ways. If we're not lucky, sometimes we die trying.

When my mom passed away, I was set adrift, but I was also set free. The invisible strings had been cut, all those scraps of paper shredded, the piles blown away by mortality's strong gust. Things were restored to order. That performing part of me, that circus animal trained to make her proud, sat down and said, "I think I'll take a break."

No more self-doubt. No more self-recrimination. No more fear that if I stopped striving, I'd fade from view or sink below the surface, never to be seen again. My mother couldn't cut me down anymore, so I no longer felt called to do the things that might make her turn away the blade.

I thought back to late last year, when we all accepted that she wasn't ever going to come back to her widow's-rest apartment in the retirement community, and it was time to clean it out and give it up.

One afternoon, I went to the nursing home, got the keys, and let myself into her place. I stood in the small foyer, the air thick with the smell of cigarette smoke and dust, unsure where to start.

I looked at the piles, overstuffed closets, heaps of kitchen mess. *Jesus, what do I do with all this stuff?*

The prayer impulse was getting more reflexive. I repeated the question: *Jesus? What do I do with all this stuff?*

I did what I knew how to do. I went to the convenience store and bought a pair of Playtex gloves—rubber ducky yellow and so completely nonporous they made my hands sweat within a minute—and started by winding my way through the rooms, tiptoeing along the goat trails, stuffing things that were clearly garbage, old junk mail, expired prescriptions, anything crusted shut or broken, into trash bags. When one bag was full, I moved on to the next, hauling two at a time to the garbage chute down the hall. I went to the chute so many times, each trip on the worn path became a mini pilgrimage. A walking meditation. In ninety minutes, I filled fifteen bags in all, and scarcely made a dent. I packed up a few things I wanted—a scarf I had sent to her as a souvenir twenty years before; a plastic-wrapped stack of unused Anthora cups, the kind you get in a city deli, blue paper bordered with a white Greek key design, and printed in gold script, "We Are Happy to Serve You" in a scroll. The sacred text of New York. Even though, judging by the surly souls pushing your coffee across the countertop, you'd never guess that the sentiment held, I've always chosen to believe in the cup.

Everything I tossed out that wasn't inarguably trash tugged at me: *What if someone wants this? Can I donate this someplace?* A little of the hoarder's anxiety rubbing off on me. I thought of the great Zen masters who teach the art of letting go of attachment. Then I thought, *You probably don't find many hoarders in monasteries.* Then I thought of the grand directive of the sages: *Before enlightenment, chop wood, carry water. After enlightenment, chop wood, carry water.* The essential tasks of life stay the same; it is only our perspective that shifts. Most of us don't get to live high on a mountaintop, sipping the golden ethers of elevated consciousness. We grow wiser in the muck and toil, the tedium and temple-throbbing crush of our everyday lives. We have to evolve in place, like the lotus that blooms in the mud. We throw out the trash even though the trash brings deep sadness. We avoid the spiral of self-blame and the dead end of questioning why it had to come to this. *Before enlightenment, bag trash, carry it down the hall. After? Ditto and Amen.*

The greatest obstacle to caring for my mother was my mother herself. All I wanted to do was help. The one thing I wasn't allowed to do was help. Now, though, now I could help, picking up and stuffing trash into the bags over my arm as if it were a divine calling.

To clean up a hoard is to trace the labyrinth of the stalled mind. Around every turn is sorrow. The sorrow of loss. The sorrow of stasis and waste. And the sagging exhaustion behind it all. I knew that as my mother's health declined, and eventually failed, that I'd keep cleaning up after her. We all would. We'd keep cleaning and culling and sorting until the only thing left was the marble box containing her ashes.

I've heard more than one sermon describing the journey the pain of others makes: into our hearts then out through our hands in acts of compassion. What a perfect way to illustrate the service of care. For a child with a mentally ill parent, you feel so often that what you do is never, ever enough. Children aren't supposed to parent their parents, but that impulse has its own heartbeat. We equate love with care. More caring means more love. But if we must learn that we can't satisfy ourselves with more—more effort, more striving, more denial, more rationalizing, more performing—we learn, also, that trying to satisfy someone mentally ill with more is equally futile, because more never ends up being enough. A little will have to do. But grace multiplies, and it magnifies too. As with bread cast upon the waters, our helpful labors are increased. A little suddenly becomes a lot, and what once seemed impossible is accomplished, the tiniest bit at a time. The miracle of grace precipitates the alchemy of loss, where sorrow flies with freedom, and mercy snaps on a brand-new pair of yellow rubber gloves.

19

⟶⟨⟶

GIRL CRUSH

I am an unrepentant flirt, but I save all that sugar for the ladies. I'm capable of complimenting men, but I don't, usually, lest it be mis-construed as an invitation. Now and then I'll say something benign to a guy I know well, like my husband's boss ("Sharp-looking polo shirt, Dave"), but the serious sweetness gets drizzled on my girl crushes. There are scores of women around me whom I admire to the point of infatuation. I admit it—I'm a bit of a floozy in this department.

Consider the subjects of my thrall: An arts-loving aviator with a PhD and exacting taste in craft beer. A yogi military policewoman— awarded four bronze stars, which she'll never tell you about—who, with her steel grey buzz cut, looks just as heart-stopping in lululemon as she does in camouflage. A hospice nurse who rescues animals and makes vegan Thin Mint cookies that taste as though they were baked by a Michelin-starred Girl Scout. A heady mixture of affection and admiration, the girl crush is God's gift to women, like the bonus at Clinique: yours to enjoy—*free!*—for enduring the challenges of womanly existence.

To me, the love between women is highest holiness. You can adore your husband to the marrow, but matrimonial love does not supplant the love for your girls. I know I'm lucky to have a true partner in my husband, but in addition to being happily married, I am a woman's woman through and through. I count on my girlfriends the way I count on nothing else—to be supported, heard, healed, and inspired—and I am honored to be relied upon the same way.

I know the litany of misogynistic dissent: "You can't trust other women." Or "Girls are too much drama." Women stab each other in the back, hold each other down, sell each other out. But in my life, the opposite has been true. For some, *sistering* can mean contagion, like a wound or a plague. For others it can mean support, like one joist bolted to another for strength. To be blessed among women, to me, is to have their companionship and devotion. Other women are my lifeblood, full stop.

My girl crushes on the famous are few and far between: Tattooed Lutheran pastor Nadia Bolz-Weber, who says that as a teenager, her Holy Trinity was David Bowie, Lou Reed, and Iggy Pop. Maya Angelou, for rising in a deeply racist literary environment to tremendous success that she unashamedly laced through with spiritual messaging. Patti Smith for all the obvious reasons.

So I didn't really know what to do when the offer I'd made to pass along a copy of a book to a noted writer on her Facebook page was met with an enthusiastic yes. She sent me her home address, and once she'd read the book, we started messaging.

Fangirl euphoria took over, and I was off to the races.

I Google-stalked her like mad—I read the stories behind her most famous works, I pored over photos of her with her ex-girlfriend, I read up on her astrological sign. (Pisces! How dreamy!)

Distraction is my drug, and I was instantly hooked. We'd meet at night online, a nice diversion after having read *Don't Let the Pigeon Drive the Bus!* to the baby for the eightieth time that week. I was still grieving my mom. We kept it friendly, chatting about everything from our favorite authors to her hot flashes.

We both hailed Springsteen as one of our greatest living poets and Rilke as indispensable, his "Go to the limits of your longing" a clarion call we both tried to heed.[1] Clean and sober for many years, she lived her redemption story and fashioned a career out of helping others on the path from recovery to unfettered creativity, beauty from ashes paying the bills. She'd found a way back to God that I thought was just magnificent. To top it all off, she's a trained chef.

Mostly, though, she wrote her way into my heart. As much as I liked her, I liked her work even more. It showed deep commitment to telling the truth, gracefully but with a chiseling edge. Every word of hers limned the brutality of life—as an addict, as an activist, as a woman who loves women. We've all experienced weaponized truth—honesty hurled with such force it does more harm than good. If you scald or ruthlessly expose or invade people in the name of "honesty," then what are you doing, exactly? Truth without tact is a blunt-force instrument, and here she was pairing honesty and tenderness as soul mates. There was a softness to her keen turn of phrase that was instructive, and with her gift for extracting beauty from darkest sorrow, she moved me deeply. I felt as though I could see clear to the aquamarine depths of her. I even gave her a nickname: Bittersweet.

A crush is a beautifully appointed blind alley. With no real way forward or through, infatuation offers a brilliant way to paw over intimacy we think we want without getting slammed with a tab we cannot pay. I'd spin cotton candy fantasies of being with her—we'd cook in her kitchen, roasting a chicken after patting its skin with flour so it came out crispy; whipping fresh cream to dollop on pecan pie hot from the oven; passing the saltcellar for a pinch to season the vinaigrette. Every once in a while, I'd dare to let myself imagine us gathering a dozen friends for a midnight feast that would ring with laughter and deep talk until the skies paled and we brewed espresso and tucked fresh-baked croissants in everyone's pockets for the ride home. The kitchen would be our platonic love den—food, drink, conversation—every luscious thing in abundance.

Then it took a turn. After a few weeks, I'd wake up craving Bittersweet, a clawing, grasping feeling at the center of my chest. I'd check my phone at four a.m., hoping for a message or two. She found me funny, and I lived for every LOL. The girl crush may not be erotic, but the pull is no less powerful—you don't want to get into her bed; you want to get into her bloodstream.

When she was scheduled to present her work in New York City, I had my hair blown out, put on a pretty dress, and rounded up four of my friends—each with her own place in my girl crush pantheon.

I feared that in person she'd be a bummer-fest of dour earnestness, but she was a nimble raconteur, a Bible Belt rebel with the delivery of a Borscht Belt yukster. She flipped through stories like a humanist shaman, shifting her delivery as she read the room, loose and funny as hell.

I brought along a small gift for her, a good luck totem she could wear as she developed a project in a new genre: a silver ID bracelet my friend Cathy had sent me to wear when I was in similar straits. On the front was engraved, "Pray daily." On the back, "Lord, give me the confidence of a mediocre white man." I stood in line with my friends after her presentation and waited for my turn to meet her. Her composure as the fans filtered by was impressive—she dispensed blessings, goodwill, and autographs left and right. No selfie was denied. I waited an hour to talk to her.

She unwrapped the bracelet from the light blue tissue paper and laughed when she read the inscription, then held out her arm and asked me to put the bracelet on her.

The next day, I sent her an effusive ten-point e-mail itemizing everything I'd enjoyed about her presentation: Her new material. Her shambling rocker style. Her hair. Her jokes. Her raw tales about her latest romantic disaster. Her obvious filial love for her fans.

I opened my messages later to find from her not words, but, for the first time, photos: What she ate for lunch on the road one afternoon. A crowd at a festival. A close-up of her wrist featuring the bracelet below the cuff of a natty, retro-styled black shirt, cuff fixed with a row of three pearlescent closures. I typed back a flirtatious response I thought both harmless and clever: "Pearl snap thirst trap. Well-played, heartbreaker."

Not long after, she went silent.

After a few days, I started feeling anxious. Deprived. Then when she showed back up, her replies didn't come fast enough or weren't long enough. She'd forget things I told her. I wasn't getting a correspondence high anymore, and it made me sad, then angry. I ached through the hours in furious withdrawal. My supply had been cut back.

As the days passed, I tried to fashion a fix by reading and re-reading our early exchanges, but this reach for her through the fence only filled me with sorrowful rage until I was brimming with the stuff. Sip honey through barbed wire long enough and it starts to taste like blood.

When something hits you so hard you're on the verge of obsession, it's time to sit quietly in prayer, because there's usually a story behind the story. I sat still and closed my eyes, tuning into the wild, straining pain in my chest. I saw the best of my mother—her driving me in the car as we went on one of our special "just us two" missions. Eating mugs of chicken noodle soup with oyster crackers she'd floated atop. Me sitting in her lap, enjoying the warmth of her body pressed against my back. I missed this part of her so acutely, her specialized affection, her kindness, I ached down to my toes. How could I not have known that maternal loss was coloring everything?

This crush, or an element of it, was trying to retrieve the irretrievable, hand over hand along the rope, trying to pull mother-love back to me. Infatuation ushered in not so much by an exorcism of Freudian demons as by the near-hysteria of deepest grief. *Don't go, don't go, don't go* was the heartbeat of my Bittersweet connection.

Some crushes, it appears, are about chasing a ghost.

And some crushes have ghosts chasing us.

I was mortified, pierced with embarrassment, when Bittersweet messaged me, asking me to dial it down. Through my flattery, I thought I was offering encouragement and affirmation. Flattery—usually darkly categorized as a feminine wile meant to ensnare—is offered among girly-girls benignly instead as a form of recognition, like, *I see you.* "You're smoking hot," means *I like you.* "You are totally fine" right back means, *I like you too.*

But Bittersweet had her own complicated history with women—particularly straight women who would yank her chain through flirting, only to pull away like Lucy with the football, sending Charlie Brown up into the air and then slamming to the ground. My thirst for connection with her, rather than being uplifting, was causing her great pain.

What could I do but apologize? Once and again. The second time I went a bit beyond, telling her five humorous, definitely unflattering things about myself. You know you're desperate to save face when you tell a woman you shave the hair on your big toes.

Bittersweet sent a quick, unadorned message back, signed off with "Happy writing." Ouch. I saw the words chiseled into a tombstone. There was no talking back to that.

I recalled one of our earliest exchanges: I had written to her, "Sometimes you don't know a limit until you cross it."

A few days later, I was surprised by a message from her. "I would just like to know: Why did you research my life? Why did you come for me? What were you hoping to get from me? I don't ask with any expectation or agenda. I'm just curious. Motivations are interesting."

I had to give her points for directness.

I closed my eyes. *God,* I asked, *what now?* I waited for that desperate feeling in the center of my chest to dissipate. From behind it came that small, still voice: "Tell the truth." With love. With gentleness. With respect for her eyes and ears and heart. The part of me that stepped forward was someone smaller and needier than I would have guessed. I wasn't sure I could move toward her on such wobbly, little-kid knees, but what did I have to lose? She was pretty much already gone. The makings of another ghost.

I flat out told her in a lengthy outpouring of the softest truth I could muster: That I was lonely. That I was grieving my mom. That I got overexcited by her interest. That flirting wasn't out of bounds in my world; it was an honest overstep, and that I assumed that as a person with a public profile, she was immune to my attention. I was sorry.

She wrote back immediately, "I like you. Can we be friends without the intrigue?"

Could I do that? I tuned in again and envisioned her looking at a ballerina in a music box, turning on pointe. With a bored and rueful smile, she gently clapped it closed and the music stopped, leaving the tiny dancing doll alone in darkness. If I wasn't on pointe, flattering and funny, was I anything to her? Jesus said, "Consider the lilies of the field, how they grow: they neither toil nor spin."[2] He lauded austerity without worry over adornment, without working to be something not required. Beauty as-is. Could I believe I had anything to offer Bittersweet as I was, without the embellishment of praise and the performance of what I'd hoped was my devastating wit? Why is it so hard for us to believe we're enough just as we are? You can polish your image any way you wish, but nothing shines like the true self.

"Listen," I wrote to her. "I know you asked me to lay off any intrigue. In exchange I ask that you not throw me away if you find you're 'done' with me. I need you to be a friend, not someone treating me like a source of one-sided uplift, then once the glitter is gone, I'm nothing."

Bittersweet responded soon after: "I will not disappear without warning, that's cruel, and I try very hard to do no harm. That would qualify as harm, I do believe. Here's the thing about boundaries: I've learned to set them in order to protect relationships so I do not have to do a disappearing act. It's an act of love, I think . . ."

In a very short space, we had asked of each other two of the most difficult things to ask another human being. *Don't hurt me. Don't leave.*

The girl crush is a wild, larking indulgence that lights in every nesting area of want—head, heart, hope, all of it. A joyous, wistful liminal state between what is and what could be, a form of endearment both adolescent and ageless in its purity. And under the right conditions—the mania of grief, the terror of loss—it can slip into something far more dangerous, an attraction and a desire for passionate friendship that blurs all bounds. Bittersweet has cemented her own special place in the pantheon, a spot in the heart made more tender for her tactful course correction, which felt like a thorn at the time but was actually a blessing.

The crush, the relationship I thought I wanted, met its end and was resurrected as something better, stronger, more true. We were no longer coconspirators in a confectionery fantasy that we could neither sustain nor justify, but equals, scraping the floor with our vulnerabilities and hearts in hand. Amateurs in the night kitchen, trying to figure out how real people blend together—a dash of raw courage, a pinch of respect sifted softly in. The baseline ingredients for friendship. That's how God moves through the girl crush, with a truth both bitter and sweet: sometimes you start out seduced by the sugar rush of infatuation, only to end up baring the salt of your soul.

20

FAMILY RECIPES

It's true that I've never had a feeling I didn't want to eat: sprinkle-topped cupcakes scarfed in a celebratory mood over birthdays and promotions, greasy slices of pepperoni pizza tossed down after disappointment. Grief is no exception. I consume so as not to be consumed.

I didn't lose my appetite when my mother passed away. I could chase the muting oblivion of any vice I could imagine, but stuck in the toadhole of loss, I accepted that I wouldn't be able to drink, drug, shop, girl crush, daydream, or overwork my way out of it. I comforted myself instead with the elemental pleasure of cooking simple things. Food is medicine for the broken heart.

I don't approach the preparation of comfort food like an urbane lady in a Nancy Meyers movie, wandering boutique market aisles stocked with colorful, locally sourced produce, fluffing a photogenic Italian parsley into the basket over my arm, then smiling as a friendly baker slides a fresh baguette into a long, white paper bag across the counter, later to be sliced for a croque monsieur made of layered artisanal Gruyère and imported prosciutto, served on a handmade stoneware plate.

I was not raised on highbrow cooking—my mother cooked quickly, making meals for seven from what she could fit into her budget, and her cart, at the local chain supermarket. For breakfast, we'd eat cinnamon toast or boxed cereal with milk. Snacks might be packaged store-brand cookies. Dinner was ready in thirty minutes max: Hamburger Helper with sliced potatoes simmering in brown beef gravy, creamy tuna casserole with canned peas mixed in, and some nameless entrees my mother improvised, like buttery mashed potatoes with hot dogs split down the middle and stuffed with melting slices of American cheese baked in a Pyrex dish. Neither fresh nor fancy ingredients are required for my satisfaction. My chef persona would be "The Payless Contessa." When I go for comfort, I go low.

Our church on Old York Road in Pennsylvania had an active choir that my sisters loved to sing with. The musicals—including a pop retelling of the story of Shadrach, Meshach, and Abednego called "Cool in the Furnace"—required long after-school practices that extended well into the evening, so dinner was served. The sloppy joes were legendary, and my mother copied down the recipe on the back of an envelope that we found tucked between the pages of Peg Bracken's *The I Hate to Cook Book* when we cleaned out her apartment.

Food has been both comfort and curse to me, and I tend to overindulge. But missing my mother made me crave those sloppy joes, so

I decided to make a batch without, for once, putting anxiety about portion control at the fore. I'd eat as little or as much as I needed to feel fed. I pulled my white Le Creuset Dutch oven from the cupboard. The heavy pot was a luxury I'd always coveted, procured at a deep discount from a local online bulletin board. I saw my mother, stooped and swaying slowly down the aisle on one of her bargain hunts at Marshall's, leaning on a shopping cart like a walker, nodding her approval.

For me, no turn in the kitchen is without self-reproach, disguised in someone else's voice as if thrown through a ventriloquist's dummy. When I bake cornbread from a mix, I hear a famous television chef say, "Really? You can't do homemade? It's just as easy," as I pour in the milk and add canned creamed corn to the batter to make it moist. While sizzling minced garlic from a jar in a pool of butter for a Bolognese sauce, I recall a gourmet sniffing about a cook who dared to live without a garlic press. One of these days I'll accept that snobs and critics are really not my concern. Even the critic who lives inside me.

Olive oil skidded in beads across the flat surface of the Dutch oven, which I'd set over a high flame. There is beauty in retracing your mother's steps in the kitchen, no matter how simply she cooked. A hand-me-down recipe is one of the great gifts of family, a connection between the generations. I browned a pound of ground beef then stirred in the sauce ingredients:

1 cup catsup
1 tablespoon white sugar
1 tablespoon brown sugar
1 tablespoon Worcestershire sauce
1 tablespoon white vinegar
1 tablespoon mustard

It had to be a homemade sloppy joe—the canned stuff is too sweet, not enough vinegary tang—and served on a soft potato roll to soak up the sauce. The sloppy joes could be made with ground turkey, even with vegetarian meat-substitute crumbles, but I craved it with old-school ground beef. When I sampled it as it cooked, I wanted to feed it to the world by the spoonful. Maybe sometime I could get crazy and toss some diced onion in there, a handful of finely chopped celery, or double the brown sugar and leave out the white, or switch the vinegar from white to apple cider—but for now I wanted the sandwich of my youth. Proust on a bun.

When the mixture had simmered for ten minutes, I stood over the stove and ate it with a serving spoon, straight from the pot.

Using my mother's recipe made me miss my father. There seemed to be a domino effect to my grief—a new loss tapping into an old loss that tapped into a loss before that, and so on, until it felt that life is but a series of abandonments. Living is so much more than losing people, but it is hard to see the good stuff—shooting stars, hugging, Twix—when death is fresh and blocks the sun.

My mother was the designated family cook, but my father was the baker. He'd make Swedish cookies like *papparkakor* and *pfeffernüsse* at Christmas, and sometimes my sister Annette would join him in the kitchen to shape marzipan fruits. Weekends, he might make waffles in an old-fashioned stove-top waffle iron constructed of two hinged cast-iron plates that turned on long stainless steel arms. When a waffle was done, the exact timing of which only he seemed able to discern, he'd separate the crispy-edged waffle from the iron with the tines of a fork and slide it onto a plate. Then it would be snatched up by one of us kids, bathed in maple syrup, and consumed at lightning speed in front of the television. What I missed most when I missed my father were cookies. Not the Swedish holiday fancies, but the Midwestern cookie jar basics: oatmeal raisin, chocolate chip, and most of all, peanut butter.

I looked online for something that resembled his peanut butter cookie recipe, but recipe websites always frustrate me. Someone will review a recipe favorably, and then comment, "This cookie is delicious! I made a few modifications, substituting rice flour for wheat flour, I omitted half of the peanut butter, added a half cup of fresh almond butter, and used egg whites instead of whole eggs. I left them in the oven ten minutes longer than the recommended baking time, as I like a crunchier cookie."

That is not a modification; that is a different recipe.

My sister had sent me the latest church cookbook from her congregation in Nebraska. I love church cookbooks, all those crazy salads with mayonnaise, and casseroles topped with potato chip crumbs or crushed cornflakes. Question the role of women in church all you want, but don't deny who's been keeping everybody fed. I felt a zing of subversive pleasure seeing this church cookbook where a female name isn't just attached to each recipe, but also atop the clerical staff page. My sister! The cookbook had a recipe for three-ingredient peanut butter cookies that looked close enough to Dad's to scratch the sentimental itch.

I measured out a cup of peanut butter and a cup of sugar. The baby walked over and hugged my leg. "Up me!" She was at the stage where she very much wanted to help, to be part of the big-kid world.

My mother had taught me how to prepare scrambled eggs when I was very young. I can certainly remember whisking eggs together with a dash of milk and listening to them bubble at the edges after pouring them into the small cast-iron skillet when I was five or six. I was a kid before bike helmets and mandatory seat belts, so a kinder-gartner in front of a gas burner was not some big deal.

I held my daughter's little hand in mine, and we rapped the egg against the rim of the glass mixing bowl until the shell fractured. We watched the egg slide down the side of the bowl into the sugar. Learning to cook is an important step toward self-sufficiency, and I wanted to start her on the basics as soon as possible.

Someday when she's grown she might ask me, "What was the first thing I learned to do in the kitchen?" and I'll tell her, "You learned to crack some eggs."

Symbolically, this pleases me.

I dropped rounded spoonfuls of cookie dough onto the baking sheet, and a huge sadness winged from me. Pressing a fork into the dough to make a crosshatch pattern brought my father back to me so vividly, I could hear him whistling through the sizable gap in his front teeth. My father. My daughter. That they'd never know each other is one of my greatest sorrows.

My father grew up in rural Ohio, and our grandmother stayed put even after her six children had moved away. We considered her house our one stable home, a small two-bedroom in the heart of Sandusky County. My grandmother, if she didn't like cooking, didn't seem to mind it. She'd make conversation while she stood peeling potatoes or apples with a paring knife at the kitchen sink, the blade sending a corkscrew of peel into the basin. A typical Sunday dinner at my grand-mother's house was baked ham loaf—which I later learned was an Amish staple; plenty of Amish and Mennonites around in rural Ohio—served straight from the baking pan, a frozen vegetable blend of lima beans, diced carrots, and peas boiled on the stove, and fresh mashed potatoes with plenty of lumps. From my seat at the kitchen table, I could read this poem on a wooden plaque hanging above her sink:

Thank God for dirty dishes;
They have a tale to tell.
While others may go hungry,
We're eating very well.
With home, health, and happiness,
I shouldn't want to fuss;
By the stack of evidence,
God's been very good to us.

I never enjoyed cooking because I was terrible at it, and I found it tiring to come up with menus, to bring focus to steaming vegetables and braising tenderloins. It's not self-expression to me. It's just another chore. But to cooks like my grandmother, the kitchen is a crucible of love.

There's a part of me, some tiny imaginary part of me, that scoots around in a frilly gingham apron and pirouettes while she vacuums, that feels—even though I generate income and support our family emotionally and practically—that I'd be a *real* mom and wife if I liked cooking—if I *wanted* to do it. And I feel guilty that I don't, the same way I feel guilty when I leave my daughter at daycare and she cries. But since I have the flexible workday, dinner prep and cleanup fall to me.

I didn't like cooking any more than my mother did. She'd turn out a nice Christmas roast beef and Thanksgiving turkey and Easter ham, and set a pretty table, but while those traditions had meaning, everyday cooking was a grind. I thought about my widowed grandmother, working full-time as a math teacher, preparing big meals for her six children, then later, her unruly pack of grandchildren, who ended up numbering eighteen. Grandma never seemed harried or self-conscious about the simple fare she prepared. That poem over her sink summed it up: my grandmother's kitchen staple was gratitude.

Before I met Mike, I knew what it was to eat tense date-night dinners with the wrong person, and to shovel down containers of leftover Chinese over the sink, alone. Being the family chef can be a bother, but it's also a privilege not to be taken for granted. When I cook now, I say a silent thank-you for having the food I need, the kitchen to prepare it in, and a family happy to eat what I offer. Chris brings his new girlfriend around, and she's a welcome addition to the table, and Mikey, who stays with us now and then to help with the baby, is the quickest potato peeler I know. He'll pull up a chair by the kitchen garbage pail, pop in his earbuds, and send a five-pound bag's worth of russet peels whizzing into the bin before the water can boil on the stove, his body bent over the task like a Delta bluesman on guitar.

Things—what to keep, what to get rid of—emerged as a matter of great importance after mom died. The five of us worked out amongst ourselves what went to whom. Someone wanted the framed Maxfield Parrish poster, someone else the small Swedish upright piano. There was a minor tussle over the old-fashioned waffle iron, and it went to Kelly after she promised we could all have waffle breakfasts together at my house. Much of the costume jewelry went to thrift store bins; the clothes, even the racks of new items still tagged and on hangers, were too saturated with cigarette smoke to be donated.

What did I want of my mother's? So much less than I might have assumed before she passed. Most of all, what I wanted was a prism through which I could see her clearly. Completely. Her lilting telephone voice and her caustic put-downs. Her love of research and learning, and her refusal to disclose or explore the pain of her own early life. Why she'd make it to every doctor's appointment, yet refuse any kind of psychiatric care, no matter how many times it was suggested. Compassion for her meant understanding that much of what she did that harmed us was beyond anything she could control. Compassion for myself meant forgiveness for needing to stay clear of the blast radius. I thought my avoiding her was a sign of weakness, but it was an act of preservation. I didn't seek to blame her; I wanted to know her.

Man, it is hard to move into being the older generation of a family. You're not orphaned, but still you are left alone, left behind. There would be no Christmas gifts for the baby to open in front of the grandparents, no shoe-tying skills to show off, no bumble-butt ballet recitals in a pink tutu and tights. And what family stories I didn't know died with my parents. A generation of witnesses, gone. What I had of them to offer my daughter was a handful of recipes, and the gratitude for having them was my task to grab with both hands.

When the peanut butter cookies were cool, I slid them from the nonstick sheet with a spatula and put them on a plate. I ate four— they were surprisingly rich and filling—then set aside the rest for the baby and for Mike. This recipe, nothing remarkable about it, was part of family lore, as inextricable as the stories that defined us, even as we talked around them, even as we ran from them. I had been terrified that the truth would harm me, or find me cast out, but in the end, it brought me home. The force to seek the truth is insistent, as strong as life itself. If there is an instinct beyond fear, it is the instinct to know.

21

SANCTUARY

One impressive feature of our human community is that we manage to keep the whole caravan rolling somehow. Rarely do we come unglued all at once; someone's usually got it together enough to keep the others on course. But once in a while—more often than I'd allow if I were in charge—something so terrible happens that everyone veers into the ditch at the same time. A cherished child falls ill or dies, and the family goes to pieces. A tornado tears through town, reducing hundreds of homes to splinters and glass shrapnel. A potentially unstable political candidate is elected into office. (I'm not mentioning any names).

What do we do when catastrophe strikes?

We seek sanctuary. With others, and within ourselves.

To effectively create sanctuary, you must first create space. To create that space, it is vital to, before anything else, admit that you're run ragged, despairing, and in need of shelter and rest. There's a spoon theory of debilitating illness: you only have so many "spoons" of energy to use in a given day when you're ill, with seven to fifteen spoons allotted for each twenty-four-hour period. The theory, developed by Christine Miserandino,[1] who suffers from lupus and other often-invisible ailments, posits that for the compromised, it can take, for example, two spoons to get out of bed, then five spoons to get through work, leaving only a few spoons of energy for the rest of the day. For the chronically ill, a quickly exhausted spoon inventory is a fact of daily life, but external events can deplete you as swiftly as any illness. Everyone's a "spoonie" sometime.

The "buck up, buttercup" urge to drive on is implanted in so many of us who were raised to be good little soldiers, and stoicism can keep you going for a long time. So can fleeing the scene, seeking refuge in the escape artistry of dissociating via daydreams or denial. But that won't work forever.

The nightmare is real. The creek keeps rising, and the pull of the current wears you down.

This is where the spiritual survival plan comes into play. It's called a spiritual practice so you're practiced for when you really need it—during depression, disaster, upheaval, loss. Step 1: admit you're lost at sea. Acceptance leads to productive, protective measures. Then, start throwing everything that isn't necessary cargo overboard, so you can paddle against that brutal current. No extraordinary people-pleasing measures; let the softball league e-mails sit another few days, and know that those clothes don't need to be folded right this second. Breathe. Stretch. Drink cold water and hot tea. Naps are a sacrament. If you can't sleep, at least get off your feet for a moment, and rest your eyes. Scientific research has proven that garbage TV has restorative properties. These seem obvious, yet they're the first things to fly out of your head when you are, as my husband says, up to your arse in alligators.

Identify, and itemize, your agents of healing, for they are your angels of healing. I wrote these things down to remind me of what I need, like a packing list. I should probably attach it to my person with a set of mitten-clips threaded through my jacket sleeves. The first thing I lose in emotional chaos is my basic recall. Is it call a water and drink some friends? No wait: drink some water and call a friend. Ah.

I remember after 9/11, my friend Fawn and I spent a night driving to and from a house full of chums and cuddly dogs while listening to Elvis Costello's "Oliver's Army" over and over, having resorted to the usual tricks: the comfort of old songs and old friends, community, conversation, and the love of loyal pets. It made us feel less helpless, less alone. The words of African-American writer Audre Lorde have lately been revived as a rebel yell: "Caring for myself is not self-indulgence, it is self-preservation, and that is an act of political warfare."[2] Of course, companies try to commodify self-care all the time ("Self-care your way to a perfect, youthful complexion with our five-hundred-dollar-a-jar moisturizer!"), but peel away the consumer come-on and the sentiment stands. And shallow as it may seem, some people find a trifle like a pedicure or a new tattoo uplifting—gold tassel trim on the battle flag. When my friend Joey's newborn son spent six weeks in the NICU, she wore sunny coral lipstick when she visited him every day, to declare to the staff and the other mothers her dearly held femme aesthetic. Some cosmetics are not cosmetic. As Kenny Mellman, half of the divine performance duo Kiki and Herb, says, "Glamour is resistance."

After the 2016 election, everyone I knew was stressed, dejected, and wringing their hands over what would come next. I was sick at heart, too, but having beaten back my depression for the time being, I had some energy to spare, so I was happy to run around being the peppy candy striper: "Take your vitamins!" "Do you want to have coffee?"

In the lotus and the mud, God dwells and abides. It's all of a piece, and everything comes around. Toni Morrison said, "If you have some power, then your job is to empower somebody else. This is not just a grab-bag candy game."[3] We are forever in pay-it-forward mode. Grace is circular. If you have the power, share the power. If you have the energy, share the energy. I was on the other side of the semicolon in my sentence, revved up and confident my story would continue. I had spoons to spare and strength to give, so I gave it. God lives in the good and the bad, and also in the give-and-take.

I was excited to go to the Women's March in New York City the day after the presidential inauguration. But then I checked the calendar—Mike would be out of town, and bringing my feral woman-child to the city, or even to the local march, would be a day-long tantrum in the making. I was housebound.

My recovery buddy Frannie gave me a beat-down for moping that I couldn't go. She found me annoyingly indulgent for being afraid that my absence equaled coming up short as an activist, as a feminist. Self-centered fear, she called it. "You seriously think that because you didn't make the exact contribution you wanted, you failed? That's bull." She coiled her silver braid atop her head and lit a cigarette.

When we think we are failures, maybe we need to take a beat and ask ourselves whom, exactly, we have failed. Maybe letting our perfectionism be the boss of us isn't the healthiest relationship.

"I wish you'd stop smoking," I told her.

"I wish you'd mind your own business." Frannie turned her head to blow a jet of smoke away from me. "God loves you," she said, "and there's nothing you can do about it."

"The spiritual life is . . . first of all a matter of keeping awake," said Thomas Merton.[4] Awake and, I'd say, alert to possibilities, even when things don't go as you'd hoped. If you can't hit the streets, you can beam out love and pray for your enemies, or people you'd planned to protest in person if you weren't at home playing "Yellow Submarine" on a Fisher-Price xylophone. So instead of getting my cheeks bitten by cold as I marched in sisterhood in what would turn out to be one of the largest protest marches in American history, I held a one-woman prayer vigil in the den, while my daughter upended her boxes of Duplos and watched *Bubble Guppies*. Praying for people doesn't mean you approve of them, enjoy their company, or support their agenda. It's not a short-term loan or a kidney. Loving and praying for someone who offends you isn't an embrace, per se. It's more like a nudge with your toe back toward the light. Let's just say I love, and pray for, a whole lot of people whom I don't really like all that much.

Again, not mentioning any names.

Millions of people around the country, around the world, took to the streets in peaceful protest. In New York City alone, an estimated half a million people marched from the United Nations down Forty-Second Street and up Fifth Avenue to Trump Tower. Friends sent along photos and videos from the march. In one clip, I heard church bells playing "Lift Every Voice and Sing"—a spiritual, mighty and beautiful, that defined the civil rights movement. I don't know why, but that got me right in the cry spot. The teenager protester in me who got locked up in the Tombs saw this act for what it was—a church showing its hand through song. It is said that prayer in action is love, and love in action is service. I'd say, too, that anger with its heart open is activism, and a protest is church on its feet. Let freedom ring.

I played "Lift Every Voice and Sing" on repeat, bombing my heart until I wept. I allowed the feelings to flow without a fight; for their transformative, nourishing power, tears are liquid grace.

My sister Annette came to the house for a visit after the local Walkway Over the Hudson march. I gave her a cup of English Breakfast and listened to her talk about the other marchers, the signs and T-shirts. She'd become someone whose company I really enjoyed, along with the other three kooks with whom I grew up. With Dad always off at work when we were kids, and Mom increasingly off the rails and consigned to the saggy couch, it was up to us as individuals to find our way, and mostly, we did: a pharmaceutical lab tech, a minister, a research chemist, an engineer, and a writer with a past so murky, running for public office would be ill-advised. An odd, but amiable, assortment.

Annette says we're so different from each other, it's as if we're a family of five only children. Yet after Mom died, the most remarkable thing happened: we got closer. Throughout the process, I noticed that we're all a little peculiar. Not wholly dysfunctional, merely a jot off-center. Human. Our common quirkiness is a sanctuary all its own.

A five-alarm crisis or loss can forge you into who you really are: someone kinder, more patient, and accepting of blessed strangeness— other people's and your own. God doesn't make mistakes, so clearly I'm meant to be this weird.

"The moment we cease to hold each other, the moment we break faith with one another, the sea engulfs us and the light goes out," wrote activist and writer James Baldwin.[5] He also said, "People can cry much easier than they can change."[6] Both are true. Our task, while we work toward healing and restoration, is not to dismiss one truth or the other but to live in the tension between them.

I've wrestled with my angry streak my whole life, and I have tried—and failed—many times to bank my fires. But maybe God kept the fight in me for good reason. We're in an age that requires what civil rights legend Senator John Lewis calls "necessary trouble." Fighting back is an act of faith. Spiritual belief lies among our most private matters, but sometimes you must stride forth into broad daylight, faith with arms akimbo. If you want to be on the right side of history, then show up for the right side of history. When horrible things in the world are happening, do the opposite of those things. Share your grilled cheese; sing the good songs. There are people passing off cruelty under the guise of Christian principles, so we're obligated to show our kindest side, to look past Right versus Left to right versus wrong. Living our spirituality out loud is how we hold on to our sense of agency, decency, humanity. And humility.

As frustrated as I may become, and as many times as I faceplant in my so-called walk with the Lord, I must never forget that as much as the church has been an institution of oppression and a front for liars and cheats, it has been an agent of liberation too. I could awfulize in the old way, but I choose to see signs of repair. I choose to see hope. I'll lay down my sword and hum a vulnerable, hopeful melody instead.

Sometimes you can't be a shoe-leather activist—you're kept from marching by physical limitations, illness, geography, work, kids. But if you aren't able to go boots-on-the-ground, you can still be there in your own way. If you can't show up in person, amplify off-site. The revolution might not be televised, but the whisper campaign can start with a forwarded e-mail, text, or tweet. Love is patient, love is kind.

Love is not passive. Like resistance, it ripples outward. When you show up for one person, say the sages, you show up for everybody. Blessed are the troublemakers.

In the blustery grey days of late winter, a few buds of inspiration poked through the frozen soil. In response to rising anti-immigrant sentiment after the election, a building in my little town on the Hudson offered space for a large sign saying "No Hate. No Fear. Everyone Is Welcome Here." Then my yoga buddy Kamel sponsored a Muslim couple who had recently come to the United States. Kamel offered them jobs in one of his restaurants on Main Street, but they needed furniture and housewares too. People lined up to donate—dressers, a dinette set, a bed, and the use of a pickup truck to haul it all home in.

I didn't know what to give them, so instead of succumbing to Pollyanna paralysis, my answer was multiple choice—a gift card for a store where they could pick out new bedding, dishes, whatever they wanted. Through the kindness of strangers, this family got everything they needed for a new life in their new country in a matter of days.

The couple was situated comfortably, and everyone who donated was happy to be of use. That's the magic of sanctuary—we don't always have to dwell in it to feel better. Just as often, we heal as we build it.

I've read a lot of texts by seekers and searchers, and listened to many plaintive anthems from the journey, that conclude with a pilgrim being left with more questions than answers.

Bummer, dude.

If we don't have any hard answers to the big mysteries, we can at least leave a breadcrumb trail of clues as to how others might navigate this confusing planet productively. If it's not too much trouble, proffer a little trinket of hope, some bauble of encouragement, a polished gem of wisdom. Even some amusement, like a hula girl for the dashboard, would be good. Something to share, however small.

If I felt guilty and lazy at the outset of my recovery for having only enough brainshare for the wisdom found in bumper stickers, memes, T-shirts, slogans, and the occasional zippy recovery bromide, I forgave myself when I saw all the Post-it notes going up in the Union Square subway station right after the election. Subway Therapy was initiated by Brooklyn artist Matthew "Levee" Chavez, who set out the notes and let people write their hearts out. A desperately disappointed city turned a commuting location into an ad hoc shrine, New Yorkers and passers-through slapping up little sticky bits of inspiration and encouragement for each other. The Post-its leapt up overnight and kept on coming, some clever, some angry, all ever-so-slight, a reminder that there is hope, even humor, in all that broken-down mess. These notes were tiny holy things, little jewels slid along a thread like a string of prayers—mala beads, a rosary.

What I'd put on a few Post-its: *Start where you are.*

Use what you have.

Do what you can.

And a little Dory from *Finding Nemo*: *Just keep swimming.*

Even when we're working hard to write the second half of a semi-colon sentence, even when we're down to one spoon, we can hold on to hope and gratitude. We can offer what little we have to each other, while looking after ourselves. We can start where we are, use what we have, and do what we can, believing that small acts of mercy and kindness create big changes. We can believe that it's true when they tell us that a broken mirror still reflects light.

22

NEVERTHELESS,
SHE PERSISTED

My mother, within her wild unpredictability, always insisted that after her death she be cremated, and she wanted her five children to spread her ashes on a pretty summer day at our old family escape, Long Beach Island. Specifically, she wanted her ashes scattered near Old Barney, the tall red-and-white lighthouse overlooking the placid, blue-grey water of Barnegat Bay. She wished for us not to grieve, but to celebrate her passing with a picnic. She was not one for funerals or melancholy. She'd been imprisoned by gloom so often. Her send-off, she told us, should be bright. Upbeat.

She died in January, and on a warm, orange-gold June evening, the five of us caravanned to Old Barney. When we got out of the car, the trees and shrubs in the dunes were alive with cardinal song. ("When a cardinal you hear, an angel is near.") Annette brought out the ashes not just of my mother, but also my father and uncle Harvey, in various containers. I think Dad would have appreciated the thrift of being brought to the scattering place in an old Tupperware. The air smelled of brine, seaweed, and cedar from the small swath of maritime forest in the dunes. A snowy egret posted herself on the algae-laced jetty rocks, jabbing her needle beak into the pebbled clusters of mussels.

The last time my mother came to Old Barney, shortly before I got pregnant, she was so tired she couldn't even get out of the rental Chrysler to enjoy it. She napped in the front seat while Kelly and I walked along the south jetty and reminisced about pillaging boxes of saltwater taffy, tucking away pink-and-white peppermint twist pieces for ourselves, and eating Good Humor ice cream bought straight from the truck, silver jingle summoning us from the sand when the driver gave the bells a shake. We jumped the quartz green waves in our Sears one-pieces, reeking of Coppertone, back when we thought SPF 8 was the heavy stuff and it was still called *suntan lotion*, not *sunscreen*, as if to court the rays, not banish them.

The five of us fed my mother, father, and uncle back to the sea, one by one. Their remains were dove grey, powdery, and finer than sand. The wind came up and blew my mother waveward in an arcing gust toward the very end of the jetty, while Harvey, when I sifted him down, foamed like soap as salt water lapped over him. My father, in characteristic fashion, flew off into the breeze with no trouble and no fanfare. Honor thy mother and father, and your nutty uncle too. Good-bye and Godspeed.

When the ashes were gone, we gathered near the bulkhead at the foot of Old Barney, the sun turning hibiscus pink then radiant orange flanged in gemstone purple as it lowered toward the horizon. People kept stopping to ask us to snap photos of them in front of this genius sunset. Then we passed our phones to a lovely Persian family and sat down on the cement wall before this tropical skyscape, lined up side by side, facing it together. It was a sentimental moment, when we could sit quietly in our own thoughts and memories, and thank our parents for keeping us on the likable, employable side of weird. We were somber but relaxed, not coiled up as we were around our mother, fearing that her mood might turn and set her off lashing and snapping. There we sat, five odd ducks in a row—departed parents and a common heart between us. We were all we had anymore.

The morning after we spread the ashes, the baby lolled in the Pack 'n Play, sweaty and slow to awaken. Her dinosaur-print pajama top was damp with perspiration. I took her into the bed with me where she clung to my neck, head resting in the crook of my shoulder. She felt warm. Mike took her temperature—103 degrees.

Mike and I drove up and down Long Beach Boulevard looking for help. The walk-in clinics were closed, so we drove off the island to the emergency room of Ocean Medical Center, where a beautiful young Nigerian doctor named Moses (wow!) tended to the baby, looking gently into her ears, nose, and throat, and diagnosing her with an ear infection—her first, and so far only, one. She was in great pain. The doctor squeezed her knees, then carefully tested her reflexes with a rubber hammer while tears ran down her scarlet cheeks.

The doctor wouldn't release the baby until her fever came down, but she refused the liquid Tylenol and antibiotic mixed in a bottle of milk. I sat on a plastic chair in the corner for two hours, holding her to me while she whimpered. The smell of the hospital brought back the memory of my mother's arms around me during one of my emergency room visits when I couldn't breathe. As I ran my fingers through my own daughter's hair, I remembered my mother gently holding a Dixie cup of water for me to drink as the nurses administered a nebulizer treatment—past and present merged in maternal hands. The angry cramp in my chest that took hold whenever I thought of my mother loosened as my daughter stopped crying and we breathed in sync, my lips in her matted curls. My mother wasn't quite right and our childhoods weren't quite right, and not having to fight the truth anymore meant that I could accept it. I was gifted the sensation of resentment being lifted from me, like shrugging out from under a dentist's lead apron. Pain had packed its bags, and forgiveness, quietly, took its place.

I understand the folly in believing that God gave my baby daughter an ear infection so I'd be postured to forgive my mother. If God won't stop a tsunami or a hurricane, why would he fiddle with my kid's inner ear to lead me to a change of heart? But I can't say for certain that wasn't exactly why, and when, it happened, either. Things transpire, and it is our duty to assign their meaning. Was my mother always there when it mattered? No. But she was there when she was able. That was not nothing.

My mother loved what she called "the thin spaces," those luminous spots where the division between earth and Spirit are slightest, and the connection between them most clear. The beach was her favorite thin space, shells in her pocket, sand between her toes. Until her death, she wore around her neck a simple silver cross on a long chain, along with my father's wedding band. She traveled with my sister Barbara to her synod school every summer she was well enough. They even did a women's retreat on the Isle of Iona, the "cradle of

Christianity" in the Scottish Inner Hebrides. Maybe mental illness was my mother's legacy, but so, in its way, was faith.

I will never know, definitively, what was wrong with her—my guess would be bipolar II in addition to the hoarding, though who could say?—but I have the clarity of vision to accept she wasn't well, and that she was also brilliant and in her own way, inspired. It is what it is, and she leaves with me who she was: a woman with a willingness to believe, despite the odds, despite her own darkness. It is, along with a broken brain, her genetic gift to me, footprints no wave can wash away whether I am carried by God, or dragged.

On the altar in my office stands my collection of flaming sacred hearts, and a black speckled stone for grounding and a pink striped stone for love. A photo of a New Jersey highway exit to New York City taken by my friend Eleni and a votive candle depicting Lemmy from Motörhead as Jesus given to me by Mary Beth when my mother died. In the center stands a statue of the Virgin Mary that I found for $1.99 in a thrift store—*Santa de Salvation Army*—her head wreathed in a crown of resin stars.

Eighteen months after a mother's death is far too early to assess her in total. The grief is still too fresh, too disorienting. I find comfort in the memory of when she returned to college to study library science the summer after I'd dropped out of high school. She went to Pitt, living alone in an apartment in a quiet neighborhood where she attended the local Presbyterian church, the same congregation as Fred Rogers of *Mister Rogers' Neighborhood* fame. She told me that Mister Rogers was as nice as you'd hope, and I can't say why, but even in the purple mohawked, multiply pierced phase I was in at the time, hearing that brought me great relief. Just a sweet little something I could believe in. Goodness you could trust, reliable and true.

As my friend Tom says, my faith has so many hedges, I could employ a full-time gardener. But one belief I hold fast is that nature speaks to us in God's voice. A month after my mother died, we five kids met at the Philadelphia Flower Show, a hyacinth-perfumed annual event she had taken us to a number of times as children. In the butterfly sanctuary, a huge blue morpho landed on my cheek, her little feet tickling my skin as she rested. We walked around together, my butterfly pal and I, for half an hour or so, until I scrunched my eyes to cue her to take flight.

Signs, to me, are enchantments that make life worth living. A wink from the Almighty. Any doubting Thomas is welcome to say they don't buy my beliefs, because, honestly, they're not for sale.

Despite my love of signs and symbols, all this time later, I'm still not a cross person. There's no Jesus fish on my car nor a sparrow inked on my skin. But this year I wanted to take ashes for Ash Wednesday, the first day of Lent, when ministers impose upon a believer's forehead the sign of the cross—two simple finger strokes of black palm leaf ash drawn as a reminder of the impermanence of this world and our own mortality.

Lent is the season of re-evaluation, reconciliation, reflection, and—here's a razzle-dazzle Christian term—repentance. For many, the word *repent* conjures images of sweat-soaked revival tent preachers swaying with hands stretched skyward, or a loon at a busy intersection carrying a cardboard sign, hollering, "Repent or the fires of hell await you!"

In our own hearts and minds, repentance is quite different from the frothy beseeching of fire-and-brimstone ministers or a wild-eyed prophet of the streets. It's not as loud, for one thing. It's more about heeding the small, still voice than yelling for the heavens.

I drew up my own list of things to sacrifice for Lent, which runs from Ash Wednesday until Maundy Thursday just before Easter—bread, distracting girl crushes, Twitter. Those were the externals. But an internal vice would be given up as well. I pledged to give up self-centered fear.

My prevailing thought for these forty days of reflection would be something other than *How badly am I going to mess this up?* The possibility of how much space that would clear inside of my head was staggering.

Ashes are a statement of faith and much more. While they symbolize our mortal limitation, they're also an invitation—to examine your most deeply held beliefs, to prompt a meaningful exchange about values, to signify transformation—and I wanted to be part of it, to be marked to honor how faith can simultaneously soften your heart and sharpen your edge.

Ashes to ashes: as life begins, so it ends, but the moments in between are what really matter, how we tend that fire inside. There's no time like the present, no day like Ash Wednesday.

Ash Wednesday was March 1. I got up early for a rainy day drive down to the city, vowing no bread, no girl crushes, no Twitter, and no self-centered fear. The commitment to giving up bread promptly fell when I stopped into a deli and couldn't resist buying an egg, cheese, and Taylor ham on a roll for breakfast. (You can take the girl out of New Jersey . . .) As for abstaining from silly girl crushes, that crumpled at the precise moment I rounded the corner in the Museum of Modern Art and nearly crashed into Rachel Maddow, who was examining a print in the Nan Goldin exhibit. I tweeted once, but the tweet was about Lent, then I immediately went back to being Lenty . . . so maybe it doesn't count as a failing?

In any case, better luck next year.

In the Ash Wednesday service at Fifth Avenue Presbyterian, the minister spoke of the meaning of Lent, of reflecting upon what it means to doubt God, to have our faith tested like Jesus' as he wandered in the wilderness for forty days. Where was God, she asked, during disasters like Hurricane Katrina? During wars and famines and terrorist attacks? God, she said, was less in these terrible events themselves, than in the love that sustained us in the aftermath. Love— which we show each other, which we welcome from God—is the grace amid the wilderness of human brutality, amid the indifference of nature. When we offer to each other the asylum of compassion and care, we are God's grace in action.

There is no day on the Christian calendar more in-your-face than Ash Wednesday. It's in your face because it's *on* your face. Taking ashes represents the awareness of the cycle of life and death, of suffering and joy, of hope borne out of darkness. A cycle I knew so intimately now. I know that I was not put in this place to peddle Jesus, like some esoteric pyramid scheme—Amway for the soul. I could only stand on this New York City street, waiting for two ministers to appear from the rain, and testify that when it came to my grand experiment in acting as if the gospel were real, I was better with than without. God doesn't give us control; God gives us choices, and I chose to believe. Pascal's Wager had paid off.

I ducked out of Fifth Avenue Presbyterian while people filtered from the pews to line up for ashes at the altar. The rain was falling softly now. I'd requested ashes to-go from two ministers who worked with Parity, an organization established to help LGBTQ people and their allies integrate identity and faith. This was the first year of their

Glitter+Ash Wednesday campaign, in which purple glitter was mixed into the traditional palm leaf ashes.

"Glitter is like love," read the Parity statement about the campaign. "It's irresistible and irrepressible. Ashes are a statement that death and suffering are real. Glitter is a sign of our hope, which does not despair. Glitter signals our promise to repent, to show up, to witness, to work. Glitter never gives up—and neither do we."[1]

I paced in wait for the ministers under the awning of Carnegie Hall, where I had not first felt God, but rather, where God had sung to me in the voices of others. A woman hurried by under an umbrella with van Gogh's *The Starry Night* printed on it. Buses sent up sprays of water as they drove through puddles on 57th Street. The self-centered fear hovered over me on nervous wings, but I refused it, just as I had rejected the rosy poison of Christian perfectionism. In my world, secular and marbled with skepticism, the controversy isn't that I'm doing faith wrong but that I'm doing it at all—that I'm willing to turn my forehead into a proclamation of belief so physical, so loudly archaic. I can't control what people think; I can only engage their opinions as I come across them. The cross as a symbol is too fraught to be taken at face value, but I can at least use it as an opportunity to explain what it means to me personally.

In the Kindle version of the Bible, the most highlighted passage is Philippians 4:6–7 (NIV): "Do not be anxious about anything, but in every situation, by prayer and petition, with thanksgiving, present your requests to God. And the peace of God, which transcends all understanding, will guard your hearts and your minds in Christ Jesus."

I'm a long way from being able to pray all my cares away. Until then, it's meds and meditation, clouds, sun, sweet, bitter, and salt, combined with the daily exercises of kitchen-sink enlightenment:

finding the sacred in the ordinary, and beauty in the dark. Faith is a muscle, and through the basic rituals of belief, I get a little stronger every day.

Ministers Marian Edmonds-Allen and Elizabeth Edman emerged like apparitions from the drizzle, in leather jackets and clerical collars. They were fresh from imposing ashes all morning at the Stonewall National Monument in the West Village. Elizabeth opened a silver jar, no larger than an inkwell, filled with dark, sparkling ashes. She stepped in close and traced her thumb down, then across, my forehead, preparing me to present to the world the face of the faithful. "Remember that you are dust, and to dust you shall return."

In a moving scene from the show *Louie*, sad sack comedian Louis C.K. asks the legendary funnywoman Joan Rivers how she managed to get back on her feet and keep going after her husband Edgar's suicide decades before. Could life after something so devastating ever seem worth living again? Louis asked. Does it get better?

Joan said, plainly, every moment of pain still etched in her expression, "It doesn't get better. You get better."[2]

Yes. That would be my own dispatch from the dark: It didn't get better. I got better. And, inevitably, it will get bad again. And I'll get better again, because I am not alone. I believe that now.

I turned away from the ministers and walked off through the streets of this city so like my life, like my ashes—a little glitter, a lot of grit. Flawed, worthy, and willing to be seen.

As for the cross, honey, it's on.

PRAYER FOR AMY: A CODA

Dear Lord,

I am reaching out to you today with my heart in pieces. Amy Bleuel, our semicolon sister, took her own life on March 23. She was thirty-one years old.

Lord, please welcome her into your arms of infinite mercy. What we seek in you is rest. Let her find it. Guide her spirit to freedom.

Lord, for those who despair in Amy's absence, I ask you to send balm by the bucketful. Bring healing and a sense of belonging to those of us who are always hanging around the edges of things.

Lord, please lead me to do good work, to help ease the pain of the suffering, especially those whose suffering lies out of sight. Please keep enough fight in me to make the necessary trouble to change this world for the better.

Lord, I went to the Shrine of the Atonement today and tucked a prayer for Amy under the feet of the Holy Mother. It doesn't feel like enough somehow. So please move me, always, to say to anyone in need of hearing it: "I love you. I see you. You may feel alone, but you are not alone. As horribly as you may ache, remember: Poet Rilke said, 'No feeling is final.' This, too, shall pass."

Lord, please let me use the strength I've found in you to carry others, to embrace the hurting, the lost, and the weary. To say to them this one thing, spoken from the center of my soul: "Friend, I have been right where you are. Friend, I will always hold space for you. Friend, please know that your sorrow is no burden. In fact, you are as light as air."

Thank you, Lord, and amen.

National Suicide Prevention Lifeline:
800-273-TALK (8255)

ACKNOWLEDGMENTS

Thanks to:

My husband, Mike, for being my North Star, advocate, and dreamboat.

Mike and Chris for the honor of being in your lives, and for allowing me to play Twenty-One in heels.

Margaret Riley King for being my agent.

Meaghan Porter and Matt Baugher at W Publishing for taking a chance on me. Editors Laura Marmor at the *New York Times,* Sarah Hepola and Andrew O'Hehir at *Salon*, Susan Brenneman at the *Los Angeles Times*, Pip Cummings at *Women in the World*, Kera Bolonik at *Dame*, and Yonat Shimron at Religion News Service for publishing my faith stories so early on.

The wonderful women at West Point Child Development Center for teaching and caring for my daughter while I wrote.

Friends Lori Doughty, Gwynn Watkins, Kristen Holt Browning, and Stacey Wacknov for reading early drafts.

And Deb, who keeps me on this Earth, half girlfriend, half guru.

NOTES

Chapter 1: Taking Flight

1. William Shakespeare, *Hamlet*, in *The Complete Works of Shakespeare,* ed. David Bevington, 5th ed. (New York: Pearson Longman, 2004), 1.5.175–76. References are to act, scene, and line.
2. Quoted in Brené Brown, *Daring Greatly: How the Courage to Be Vulnerable Transforms the Way We Live, Love, Parent and Lead* (New York: Gotham Books, 2012), 150.
3. Emily Dickinson, "'Hope' Is the Thing With Feathers," *The Poems of Emily Dickinson*, ed. R. W. Franklin (Cambridge, MA: The Belknap Press of Harvard University Press, 1999), 140.

Chapter 2: The Positive Sound

1. Allen Ginsberg, "Howl, Part I," *Collected Poems 1947–1980* (New York: Harper & Row, 1984).
2. *The Black Sheep* was cast in bronze and mounted on First Avenue between First Street and Houston as a public art installation in 1990. The poem was also read by Finley at events throughout New York City.
3. Bo Young, Dan Vera, and Andrew Ramer, "Gay Eminences: A White Crane Conversation with Malcolm Boyd and Mark Thompson," MarkThompsonGaySpirit.com. The website is now defunct but can be

accessed via the Internet Archive Wayback Machine's archive of the site
from August 17, 2016, at http://web.archive.org/web/20160711040132
/http://markthompsongayspirit.com/interview3.html.

Chapter 3: Bad Christians and Other Good People

1. Chuck Lorre, Bill Prady, Lee Aronsohn, Steven Molaro, Steve Holland,
and Maria Ferrari, "The Lunar Excitation," *The Big Bang Theory*, season 3,
episode 23, directed by Peter Chakos, aired May 24, 2010 (Burbank, CA:
Warner Home Video, 2010), DVD.
2. Roxane Gay, *Bad Feminist: Essays* (New York: Harper Perennial, 2014), xi.
3. Robert M. Pirsig, *Zen and the Art of Motorcycle Maintenance: An Inquiry into
Values* (New York: Harper Perennial Classics, 2000), 304.
4. Frederick Buechner, *Beyond Words: Daily Readings in the ABC's of Faith*
(San Francisco: HarperSanFrancisco, 2004), 59.

Chapter 4: Holy Day

1. Alexander Chee, "Girl," in *The Best American Essays 2016*, eds. Jonathan
Franzen and Robert Atwan (Boston: Houghton Mifflin Harcourt, 2016),
26.
2. Michael Lipka, "5 Facts About Prayer," *Pew Research Center*,
May 4, 2016, http://www.pewresearch.org/fact-tank/2016/05
/04/5-facts-about-prayer/.
3. Emily Dickinson, "If your Nerve, deny you," *The Poems of Emily Dickinson*,
ed. R. W. Franklin (Cambridge, MA: The Belknap Press of Harvard
University Press, 1999), 147.
4. Carlyle Murphy, "Lesbian, gay and bisexual Americans differ from general
public in their religious affiliations," *Pew Research Center*, last modified
May 26, 2015, accessed April 30, 2017, http://www.pewresearch.org
/fact-tank/2015/05/26/lesbian-gay-and-bisexual-americans-differ-from
-general-public-in-their-religious-affiliations/.
5. A version of this essay originally appeared as Lily Burana, "For a
Grown-Up Goth, Halloween Is the Most Wonderful Time of the Year,"
New York Times Live, October 29, 2015, http://nytlive.nytimes.com
/womenintheworld/2015/10/29/at-halloween-reflections-on-the
-spirits-of-the-season/.

Chapter 5: Box of Terrors

1. Tim Keller, sermon, Redeemer Presbyterian Church, New York, NY, September 2013.
2. Leo Tolstoy, *War and Peace*, trans. Rosemary Edmonds (London: Penguin, 1982), 885.

Chapter 6: Joyful Noise

1. Henry Giles, "Henry Giles," *Forty Thousand Quotations: Prose and Poetical*, ed. Charles Noel Douglas (Garden City, New York: Halcyon House, 1917), Bartleby.com, last modified 2012, accessed April 30, 2017, http://www.bartleby.com/348/authors/205.html.
2. Lori Grisham, "Semicolon tattoos raise awareness about mental illness," *USA Today Network*, last modified July 9, 2015, accessed April 30, 2017, https://www.usatoday.com/story/news/nation-now/2015/07/09 /semicolon-tattoo-mental-health/29904291.
3. The website for Project Semicolon has undergone some changes in the wake of Amy Bleuel's untimely and tragic death, so these quotations are no longer a part of the site's content. But for current content and updates on the global nonprofit, visit http://projectsemicolon.org.

Chapter 7: Self-Improvement for Jerks

1. Glennon Doyle Melton, Twitter post, July 15, 2015, http://twitter.com /GlennonDoyle.
2. Thema Bryant-Davis, Twitter post, April 30, 2017, https://twitter.com /drthema.
3. Russell Simmons, Twitter post, July 28, 2012, http://twitter.com /UncleRUSH.

Chapter 8: The Ned Flanders Effect

1. "Religion Among the Millennials," *Pew Research Center*, last modified February 17, 2010, accessed April 30, 2017, http://www.pewforum .org/2010/02/17/religion-among-the-millennials.
2. "Ku Klux Klan," *SPLC: Southern Poverty Law Center*, accessed April 30, 2017, https://www.splcenter.org/fighting-hate/extremist-files/ideology /ku-klux-klan.

3. "CIA Interrogations: The ends justify the means," *Washington Post* infographic, last modified December 16, 2014, accessed April 30, 2017, http://apps.washingtonpost.com/g/page/politics/washington-post -abc-news-poll/1514.

4. John Fugelsang, Twitter post, March 27, 2013, http://twitter.com /JohnFugelsang.

5. Much of the material in this section was previously published in Lily Burana, "Don't Judge Me for My Jesus Memes," *Los Angeles Times*, May 1, 2016, http://www.latimes.com/opinion/op-ed/la-oe-burana-christian -progressive-20160501-story.html.

Chapter 9: The Glitter High

1. Ram Dass, *One-Liners: A Mini-Manual for a Spiritual Life* (New York: Bell Tower, 2002), 13.

Chapter 11: This Is My Body

1. Flannery O'Connor, "To Elizabeth and Robert Lowell," *The Habit of Being: Letters of Flannery O'Connor*, ed. Sally Fitzgerald (New York: Farrar, Straus and Giroux, 1979), 57.

Chapter 12: The Isle of Mom

1. Sylvia Plath, *The Bell Jar* (New York: HarperCollins, 2003), 24.

Chapter 13: This Is My Blood

1. Cindy Wooden, "Have the Courage to Marry, Start a Family, Pope Tells Youths in Assisi," *Catholic News Service*, last modified October 4, 2013, accessed April 30, 2017, http://www.catholicnews.com/services /englishnews/2013/have-the-courage-to-marry-start-a-family-pope-tells -youths-in-assisi.cfm.

2. Francis X. Rocca, "Pope, in Philippines, Says Same-Sex Marriage Threatens Family," *Catholic News*, last modified January 16, 2015, accessed April 30, 2017, http://www.catholicnews.com/services /englishnews/2015/pope-in-philippines-says-same-sex-marriage -threatens-family.cfm.

Chapter 14: Letter to My (Possible) Son

1. This quote appears in one of Kerouac's journal entries that was viewable during a New York Public Library exhibit of his life and works. See David Zahl, "Jack Kerouac and the Grave Fault," *Mockingbird*, last modified January 22, 2008, accessed April 30, 2017, http://www.mbird .com/2008/01/jack-keroauc.

2. Leelah's note originally appeared on her Tumblr blog but has since been deleted. The full text has been preserved in J. Bryan Lowder, "Listen to Leelah Alcorn's Final Words," *Slate*, last modified December 31, 2014, accessed April 30, 2017, http://www.slate.com/blogs/outward /2014/12/31/leelah_alcorn_transgender_teen_from_ohio_should_be _honored_in_death.html.

3. An earlier version of this material originally appeared in Lily Burana, "Letter to My (Possible) Son," *Dame*, January 5, 2015, https://www .damemagazine.com/2015/01/05/letter-my-possible-son.

Chapter 15: Catholic Girls Do It Better

1. Chris Abani, "On Humanity," TED Talk transcript, July 2008, https://www.ted.com/talks/chris_abani_muses_on_humanity /transcript?language=en.

Chapter 16: Foxholes

1. Paraphrased from e.e. cummings, "[i carry your heart with me(i carry it in]," *Complete Poems: 1904–1962*, ed. George J. Firmage (New York: Liveright, 1991), 776.

2. Yolo Akili Robinson, Twitter post, April 15, 2017, https://twitter.com /YoloAkili.

Chapter 18: Stuff

1. Gregory L. Jantz, "The Psychology Behind Hoarding," *Psychology Today*, last modified September 5, 2014, accessed April 30, 2017, https://www.psychologytoday.com/blog/hope-relationships/201409 /the-psychology-behind-hoarding.

2. Tina Fey, Kay Cannon, Tami Sagher, and Donald Glover,

"Do-Over," *30 Rock*, season 3, episode 1, directed by Don Scardino, aired October 30, 2008 (Universal City, CA: Universal Studios, 2009), DVD.

3. Alice Schroeder, *The Snowball: Warren Buffett and the Business of Life* (New York: Bantam, 2009), 556.

Chapter 19: Girl Crush

1. Rainer Maria Rilke, *Rilke's Book of Hours: Love Poems to God*, trans. Anita Barrows and Joanna Macy (New York: Riverhead, 2005), 119.
2. Matthew 6:28.

Chapter 21: Sanctuary

1. Christine Miserandino, "The Spoon Theory," ButYouDon'tLookSick.com, 2003, https://butyoudontlooksick.com/articles/written-by-christine/the-spoon-theory/, accessed May 9, 2017.
2. Audre Lorde, *A Burst of Light: Essays* (Ithaca, New York: Firebrand Books, 1988), 131.
3. Pam Houston, "The Truest Eye," *O, The Oprah Magazine*, November 2003, http://www.oprah.com/omagazine/toni-morrison-talks-love/all.
4. Thomas Merton, *Contemplative Prayer* (Garden City, NY: Image Books, 1971), 29.
5. Richard Avedon and James Baldwin, *Nothing Personal* (New York: Dell, 1964), n.p.
6. Robert Coles, "James Baldwin Back Home," *New York Times*, July 31, 1977, http://www.nytimes.com/books/98/03/29/specials/baldwin-home.html.

Chapter 22: Nevertheless, She Persisted

1. "Glitter+Ash," *Parity*, March 1, 2017, http://parity.nyc/glitter-ash-wednesday.
2. Louis C.K., "Joan," *Louie*, season 2, episode 4, directed by Louis C.K., aired July 14, 2011, (Beverly Hills, CA: 20th Century Fox, 2011), DVD.

ABOUT THE AUTHOR

Lily Burana is the author of the memoirs *I Love a Man in Uniform: A Memoir of Love, War and Other Battles*, which won the ELLE Magazine Reader's Prize, and *Strip City: A Stripper's Farewell Journey Across America*, a Best Book of the Year selection in several publications, including *Entertainment Weekly*, *Salon*, and *New York Newsday*, as well as the novel *Try*. She is the coeditor of the anthology *Dagger: On Butch Women*. Her writing on faith has appeared in the *New York Times*, the *Washington Post*, the *Los Angeles Times*, and in syndication through the Religion News Service. She lives in New York with her family. Connect with her at www.lilyburana.com.